The Best of

GEORGE
MACDONALD

HONOR
CLASSICS

The Best of

GEORGE
MACDONALD

120 DAILY DEVOTIONS
to NURTURE YOUR SPIRIT *and*
REFRESH YOUR SOUL

Edited and Compiled by Stephen W. Sorenson

HONOR **HB** BOOKS

Inspiration and Motivation for the Seasons of Life

COOK COMMUNICATIONS MINISTRIES
Colorado Springs, Colorado • Paris, Ontario
KINGSWAY COMMUNICATIONS LTD
Eastbourne, England

Honor® is an imprint of
Cook Communications Ministries, Colorado Springs, CO 80918
Cook Communications, Paris, Ontario
Kingsway Communications, Eastbourne, England

THE BEST OF GEORGE MACDONALD
© 2006 by Cook Communications Ministries

Cover Design: Jackson Design CO, LLC/Greg Jackson

First Printing, 2006
Printed in the United States of America

1 2 3 4 5 6 7 8 9 10 Printing/Year 10 09 08 07 06

Editor's note: The selections in this book have been "gently modern-
ized" for today's reader. Words, phrases, and sentence structure have
been updated for readability and clarity; new chapter headings and
Scripture verses have been combined with excerpts from George
MacDonald's text. Every effort has been made to preserve the integrity
and intent of MacDonald's original writings. Reflection questions at the
end of each reading have been included to aid in personal exploration
and group discussion.

ISBN-13: 978-1-56292-425-6
ISBN-10: 1-56292-425-7

LCCN: 2005910885

A Man of Letters,
A Man of Faith

George MacDonald—the Scottish novelist, poet, clergyman, and author of many beloved children's stories—once wrote, "You've got to save your own soul first and then the souls of your neighbors, if they will let you. And for this reason you must cultivate, not a spirit of criticism, but the talents that attract people to the hearing of the Word of God."

MacDonald understood well what his own talents were, and he used them effectively to draw people to God. Though he was involved in various ministry endeavors throughout his life, including pastorates, it was his storytelling abilities and linguistic mastery that he employed so powerfully, thus serving his Master through his God-given creative gifts.

Born in 1824 at Huntley, West Aberdeenshire, MacDonald attended local schools and went on to Aberdeen University, where he studied chemistry and natural philosophy. This was followed by three years of tutoring in London, after which he studied for the Congregationalist ministry at Independent College, Highbury. He was called to pastor Trinity Congregational Church at Arundel in 1850, but his ministry there was unsatisfactory to himself and his congregation. It seems that he did not emphasize dogma and the harsher strains of theology enough to suit the strict and stern parishioners. MacDonald resigned, apparently by mutual consent, and moved on to other ministerial duties in Manchester. From there, he went to Algiers for the sake of his health, which was frail for most of his life.

Returning to London some time later, he taught at the University of London and served as editor of *Good Words for the Young*. It was during this period that he resolved to become a professional author. Though he would continue to preach regularly (without official affiliation to a church or organization), he applied his spiritual and creative gifts to writing, seeking an outlet for his twin passions: literature and ministry. Early works—including *Within and Without* (1856), *Poems* (1857), and *Phantastes* (1858)—met with moderate success, but it was his novels of Scottish country life that earned him notoriety. These included *David Elginbrod* (1862), *Alec Forbes* (1865), and *Robert Falconer* (1868). In 1872–73, he embarked on a well-received lecture tour in America, where he met Ralph Waldo Emerson and Mark Twain, both of whom would become friends of his.

His reputation continued to grow, and he became acquainted with many of the top literary figures of the day, including Charles Dickens, Anthony Trollope, and Alfred Lord Tennyson. MacDonald also served as a mentor to Lewis Carroll, author of *Alice in Wonderland*. It was MacDonald's guidance, along with the enthusiastic response from his children, that convinced Carroll to publish the whimsical tale, which went on to become one the greatest children's classics of all time. MacDonald's own stories for children—*At the Back of the North Wind, The Princess and the Goblin, The Princess and Curdie, The Light Princess*, and numerous others—solidified his reputation as a great man of letters. Most of his fairy tales and fantasy stories are still in print and much loved by readers today, both young and old.

"I write not for children," MacDonald once said, "but for the childlike, whether they be five, or fifty, or seventy-five."

As a writer, storyteller, and thinker, MacDonald had profound influence on many of his contemporaries as well as later writers. For instance, his works inspired deep admiration among such notables as W. H. Auden, J. R. R. Tolkien, and Madeleine L'Engle. G. K. Chesterton cited *The Princess and the Goblin* as a book that had "made a difference to my whole existence." One of MacDonald's most enthusiastic admirers was C. S. Lewis, who picked up a copy of *Phantastes* one day in a train station and quickly devoured the novel. "A few hours later," Lewis recalled, "I knew I had crossed a great frontier."

Lewis later wrote of MacDonald's influence on him: "I have never concealed the fact that I regarded him as my master; indeed I fancy I have never written a book in which I did not quote from him."

For all the accolades and admiration MacDonald's work brought him, his was often a life of artistic struggle rather than ease and comfort. Married to the former Louisa Powell and with eleven children to support, MacDonald found that his reputation as a writer did not always bring commensurate financial rewards. For many years—especially the early years as an up-and-coming author—lack of money created real hardship. Those were lean years, he would later recount, that taught him to trust God for his "daily bread." Fortunately, he drew the attention of Lady Byron, who befriended him and offered financial support. Later in his life, he was given a government pension at the direction of Queen Victoria.

Besides times of financial privation, there were other hardships as well. One of the MacDonald daughters took ill during childhood, prompting her parents to move the family to the warm climate of Italy. But alas, the move did not have the hoped-for results, and the girl died. This was a devastating loss, which taught the author much about grief and suffering. Ironically, it was during the Italian sojourn in attempt to help his daughter that George realized his own weak health became much improved there. Consequently, the MacDonalds spent the better part of the next twenty years (1881–1902) in Bordighera, Italy.

Many accounts reveal that MacDonald's personality had a melancholy tinge, perhaps owing to his artistic temperament, but he could also be quite lively and entertaining. At his home in Bordighera, which he named Casa Coraggio, the large and energetic MacDonald household, along with a steady stream of guests, frequently held homespun theatrical productions and impromptu literary readings. Many happy and productive years passed, as MacDonald and his brood split their time between Italy and England.

Louisa MacDonald died in 1902, a year after celebrating their golden wedding anniversary. Three years later (1905)

George passed away, following an extended illness. Though he died in Ashstead, England, he was buried in Bordighera, where his wife had been laid to rest.

A man of devout faith and enormous literary talent, MacDonald did indeed draw many people to Christ— sometimes through his gentle and thought-provoking stories, sometimes through his forceful spoken or written sermons. An esteemed man of letters, MacDonald wanted first and foremost to be known as a devout and dedicated man of God.

The Gift of the Present Moment

—◦◦◦—

"Do not worry about tomorrow,
for tomorrow will worry about its own things."

MATTHEW 6:34

The next hour, the next moment, is as much beyond our grasp and as much in God's care as that a hundred years away. Care for the next minute is just as foolish as care for tomorrow or for a day in the next thousand years. In neither can we do anything; in both God is doing everything. Those claims only of tomorrow that have to be prepared today are the duty of today; the moment that coincides with work to be done is the moment to be minded; the next is nowhere until God has made it.

If a man sets out to do the immediate duty of the moment, wonderfully little forethought will be necessary. The only forethought required is to determine duty and pass into action. To the foundation of yesterday's work well done, the work of tomorrow will be sure to fit. Work done is of more consequence for the future than the foresight of an archangel.

Reflection

What has God called you to do today? Why is it so important for you to do your work well? Which necessary duty have you put off doing?

2

Contentment through God

"Godliness with contentment is great gain."
1 TIMOTHY 6:6

No one can have the consciousness of God and not be content. In other words, a person who does not have the Father, so as to be eternally content in Him alone, can possess a sunset or a field of grass or a mine of gold or the love of a fellow creature according to its nature—in the eternal way of inheriting, having, and holding. He who has God has all things.

To every person on earth, I say, if you are not content, it is because God is not with you as you need Him, not with you as He would be with you, as you must have Him. You need Him as your body never needed food or air, need Him as your soul never hungered after joy, peace, or pleasure.

Reflection

Why is contentment so difficult to attain in our day and age? Why can true and eternal contentment only come from God, your Creator?

3

The First Shall Be Last

"If anyone desires to be first, he shall be last of all and servant of all."
MARK 9:35

What is the kingdom of Christ? A realm of love, trust, and service. The King is the chief servant in it. Jesus said, "The rulers of the Gentiles lord it over them [yet] it shall not be so among you.... The Son of Man did not come to be served, but to serve" (Matt. 20:25–26, 28). The great Workman is the great King, laboring for His own. He who would be greatest among them and come nearest to the King must be the servant of all.

If to enter into the kingdom we must become children, the spirit of children must pervade throughout, from lowly subject to lowliest king. The lesson added by St. Luke is, "For he who is least among you all will be great" (9:48). And St. Matthew recorded, "Whoever humbles himself as this little child is the greatest in the kingdom of heaven" (18:4). Hence the sign that passes between king and subject. The subject kneels in homage to the kings of the earth; the heavenly King takes His subject in His arms. This is the sign of the kingdom between them. This is the all-pervading relation of the kingdom.

Reflection

What, specifically, does it mean to be a servant? How does God's view of who is greatest differ from many people's views?

4

Beauty Reveals God's Goodness

"The LORD is the great God, and the great King above all gods. In His hand are the deep places of the earth; the heights of the hills are His also. The sea is His, for He made it; and His hands formed the dry land."

PSALM 95:3–5

All lovely sights tend to keep the soul pure, to lift the heart up to God. The senses filled with the delights and splendor of creation reveal to us hints of His majesty, goodness, and love.

Whatever is beautiful is of God, and it is only ignorance or a low condition of heart and soul that does not prize what is beautiful. If I had a choice between two mills, one that would set fine dinners on my table, and one that would show me lovely sights in earth and sky and sea, I know which I should count the more useful.

Reflection

Think about several beautiful things in your life, and thank God for them. When can you take a little time to focus on small but beautiful things around you?

The Spirit Guides Our Prayers

"When He, the Spirit of truth, has come, He will guide you into all truth."
JOHN 16:13

I doubt if a person filled with the Holy Spirit can ask anything of God that is bad. Surely, one who has begun to pray to Him senses the bad from the good and dares not pray for that.

If you refer me to David praying such fearful prayers against his enemies, I answer that you must read them by your knowledge of the man himself and his history. He was someone with a passionate and burning heart, befitting his heritage, culture, and temperament. Yet when his greatest enemy was given into his hands, he did not take the full vengeance that he might have; instead, he contented himself with cutting off the skirt of Saul's garment. It was justice and righteousness that he craved in his soul, although his prayers took a wild form. God heard him, and gave him what contented him.

Reflection

Do you agree with MacDonald, who doubts that a believer filled with the Holy Spirit can ask God for anything bad? Do you sense that the Spirit guides your prayers?

6

Attend to the Small Things

*"Behold, You desire truth in the inward parts,
and in the hidden part You will make me to know wisdom."*

PSALM 51:6

The things most readily to be done—those that lie not at the doorstep but on the very table of a man's mind—are often the most neglected and overlooked. Can a man become strong in righteousness without learning to perform ordinary acts of kindness for his neighbor? Will a man climb the last flight of the stair when he has never set foot on the lowest step? Could it be that the Lord, who demands high virtue of us, tests us first in little tasks before he entrusts to us bigger ones?

He who demonstrates love in the small things demonstrates love in all things. He who will do it only in great things, who neglects "small" acts and tasks, does not truly understand the nature of God's love.

Reflection

What are some of the "small things" you can attend to in God's name? What's the relationship between performing ordinary acts of kindness and understanding God's love?

7

Our Loving King

*"Jesus said, 'Let the little children come to Me,
and do not forbid them; for of such is the kingdom of heaven.'"*

MATTHEW 19:14

God is simply and altogether our friend, our father, our infinite and perfect God. Grand and strong beyond all that human imagination can conceive of mighty deeds and kingly action, He is also delicate beyond all that human tenderness can conceive. With Him all is simplicity of purpose, meaning, effort, and end—namely, that we should be as He is, think the same thoughts, mean the same things, possess the same blessedness. It is so plain that anyone may see it, everyone ought to see it, everyone will see it. He is utterly true and good to us.

How terribly, then, have some theologians misrepresented God in the measures of the low and showy, not the lofty and simple qualities. Nearly all of them represent Him as a great King on a grand throne, thinking how grand He is and making it the business of His being and the end of His universe to keep up His glory, wielding the bolts of a Jupiter against those who take His name in vain.

Brother, sister, have you found our King? There He is, kissing little children and drawing them to Himself with utmost affection. There He is at a table with the head of a fisherman lying on His bosom, and somewhat heavy at heart that even he, the beloved disciple, cannot yet understand Him well. The mothers and fathers who show the greatest care, compassion, and sympathy for their children are but an earthly representation of our all-loving God.

Reflection

What is your mental picture of God? In what ways do you think God's character has been misrepresented to you?

8

Gaining Christ's Heart for Humanity

"Jesus, perceiving the thought of their heart, took a little child and set him by Him, and said to them, 'Whoever receives this little child in My name receives Me; and whoever receives Me receives Him who sent Me.'"

LUKE 9:47–48

To receive the child because God receives it, or for its humanity, is one thing; to receive it because it is like God, or for its childhood, is another. The former will do little to destroy ambition. Alone it might argue only a wider scope to it, because it admits all men to the arena of the strife. But the latter strikes at the very root of emulation.

When we receive the child in the name of Christ, the very childhood that we receive to our arms is humanity. We love its humanity in its childhood, for childhood is the deepest heart of humanity—its divine heart; and so in the name of the child we receive all humanity. Therefore, although the lesson is not about humanity, but about childhood, it returns upon our race, and we receive our race with wider arms and deeper heart.

Reflection

What does it mean, figuratively, to embrace people around us in the name of Christ?

9

Challenges on the Way to the Kingdom

"Jesus answered again and said to them, 'Children, how hard it is for those who trust in riches to enter the kingdom of God! It is easier for a camel to go through the eye of a needle than for a rich man to enter the kingdom of God.'"

MARK 10:24–25

Calling the disciples first to reflect on the original difficulty for every man to enter God's kingdom, Jesus reasserts in yet stronger phrase the difficulty of the rich man. It always was, and always will be, hard to enter the kingdom of heaven. It is hard even to believe that one must be born from above—must pass into a new and unknown consciousness. How hard? As hard as the Master of salvation could find words to express: "If anyone comes to Me and does not hate … his own life also, he cannot be My disciple" (Luke 14:26). And the rich man must find it harder than another to hate his own life. There is so much associated with it to push out the self of his consciousness that the difficulty of casting it from him as the mere ugly shadow of the self God made is vastly increased.

None can know how difficult it is to enter the kingdom of heaven except those who have tried—tried hard and not ceased to try. I care not to be told that one may pass at once into all possible sweetness of assurance; it is not assurance I desire, but the thing itself; not the certainty of eternal life, but eternal life.

I care not what other preachers may say while I know that in St. Paul the Holy Spirit and the flesh were in frequent strife. They only know how hard it is to enter into life who are in conflict every day, are growing to have this conflict every hour—no, beginning to see that no moment is life without the presence that makes strong. Though we receive salvation by grace, we struggle to live up to that high standard and calling that makes us worthy of the kingdom.

Reflection

What kinds of conflict will we experience as we seek, every day, to pursue life with God? As we seek to be holy, what obstacles will we face? Why do the Spirit and the "flesh" battle constantly?

Rest Is God-Ordained

"Yes, you will lie down and your sleep will be sweet."
PROVERBS 3:24

No one can deny the power of the wearied body to paralyze the soul. But let me posit a correlate theory: While the body wearies the mind, it is the mind that restores vigor to the body. The mind and heart, in sleep, come into a less disturbed contact with the peaceful, genuine source of creation. With daily troubles dissipated, one comes to drink deeply at the fount of living water, and gifted with calmness and strength, the soul is able to impart comfort and restoration to the weary frame.

The cessation of labor affords but the necessary occasion—makes it possible, as it were—for the occupant of an outlying station in the wilderness to return to his Father's house for fresh supplies to sustain life and energy. The worker goes home at night and returns in the morning to the labors of the field. Mere physical rest could never on its own build up the frame in such light and vigor as come through sleep. The heart and mind must rest, too, and thus be supplied for the work ahead.

Reflection

What is the connection between rest and spiritual vigor? Many people in our society are sleep deprived and suffer accordingly. Do *you* receive enough sleep?

God in Human Form

"[Jesus], being in the form of God, did not consider it robbery
to be equal with God, but made Himself of no reputation, taking
the form of a bondservant, and coming in the likeness of men."

PHILIPPIANS 2:6–7

D o you believe in the Incarnation—God in all His holy
might coming to earth as a man? If you do, let me ask further: Was Jesus ever less divine than God? My answer to my
own question is, "No, never." He was lower, but never less
divine. Was He a child then? Yes, but not like other children. I
say He was a child, whatever more He might be. God is man and
infinitely more. Our Lord became flesh, but did not become
man—not in the way we typically think of man. He took on
Himself the form of man: He was man already. And He was, is,
and ever shall be divinely childlike. He could never have been a
child if He could ever have ceased to be a child.

Let us dare, then, to climb the height of divine truth to
which this truth of our Lord would lead us: God became a
child for our sake. Does it not lead us to conclude that the
devotion of God to His creatures is perfect? That He does
not think about Himself but about us? That He wants nothing for Himself, but finds His blessedness in the outpouring
of blessedness?

We will draw near with our human response, our abandon-
ment of self, in the faith of Jesus. He gives Himself to us—will

we not give ourselves to Him? Will we not give ourselves to each other, whom He loves?

Reflection

What would inspire God, enthroned in heaven, to become a child on earth? Think about what motivated Jesus to come to earth and become a child, and why He has such deep love for children.

12

God's Majesty and Simplicity

———

"Now, O LORD, You are our Father."
ISAIAH 64:8

The God who ever expresses Himself in the profusions of nature; who takes millions of years to form a soul that will understand Him and be blessed; who never needs to be, and never is, in haste; the God of music, painting, mountains, and oceans; the God of history working in time unto Christianity; this God is the God of little children, and He alone can be perfectly, unreservedly simple and devoted.

Our longing desires can no more exhaust the fullness of the treasures of the Godhead than our imagination can touch their measure. Of Him not a thought, not a joy, not a hope of one of His creatures can pass unseen; and while one of them remains unsatisfied, He is not Lord over all.

Therefore, with angels and archangels, with spirits of the just made perfect, with little children of the kingdom, indeed, with the Lord Himself, and for all those who know Him not, we praise, magnify, and laud His name in itself, saying, "Our Father."

Reflection

What does it reveal about God that He is simultaneously majestic and simple? Praise God the Father for who He is and His deep love for you that is expressed in so many ways.

13

Faith and Miracles

———◆◆◆———

*"You seek Me, not because you saw the signs, but because
you ate of the loaves and were filled. Do not labor
for the food which perishes, but for the food which endures to
everlasting life, which the Son of Man will give you."*

JOHN 6:26–27

Those miracles that revealed Christ's character to those who already had faith in Him, He would not do where unbelief predominated. He often avoided crowds and declined mighty works because of unbelief. Except for the loving help His miracles gave the distressed, revealing Him as Redeemer, He may not have performed a single one. I do not think He cared much about them. Certainly, He did not expect much to result from those mighty deeds. A mere marvel is soon forgotten; inward sight alone can convince of truth; signs and wonders never.

No number of signs can do more than convey a probability that He who displays them is who He says He is. They cannot convey the truth. But the vision of the truth itself, something altogether beyond the signs and wonders, is the real power of God. It is the power that brings salvation.

Reflection

Why don't the effects of miracles last in people's minds and hearts? What happens when we expect God to do miracles yet do not seek to know Him and His salvation?

Some Suffering Is Useful

"We also glory in tribulations, knowing that tribulation produces perseverance; and perseverance, character; and character, hope."

ROMANS 5:3–4

There are tenderhearted people who virtually object to the whole scheme of creation. They would neither have force used or pain suffered. They talk as if kindness could do everything, even where it is not felt. Millions of human beings but for suffering would never develop an atom of affection. The man who would spare *due* suffering is not wise. It is folly to conclude a thing ought not to be done because it hurts. There are powers to be born, creations to be perfected, and sinners to be redeemed through the ministry of pain that could be born, perfected, and redeemed in no other way.

Reflection

What have you learned as a result of suffering and its resulting pain? How might God want you to use what you have learned through suffering to help other people?

God Cannot Contradict Himself

"Our God is a consuming fire."

HEBREWS 12:29

That man is perfect in faith who can come to God in the utter dearth of his feelings and desires, with the weight of low thoughts, failures, neglects, and wandering forgetfulness, and say to Him, "You are my refuge because You are my home." Such a faith will not lead to presumption. The man who can pray such a prayer will know better than another that God is not mocked; that tears and entreaties will not work on Him to the breach of one of His laws; that for God to give a man because he asked for it that which was not in harmony with His laws of truth and right would be to damn that man—to cast him into the outer darkness. And he knows that out of that prison the just, imperturbable God will let no man come until he has paid every cent.

If the man should forget this, the God to whom he belongs does not forget it, does not forget him. Life is no series of chances with a few providences sprinkled between to keep up a justly failing belief; life is the unfolding providence of God. The man will not live long before life itself will remind him. It may be in agony of soul, of that which he has forgotten. When he prays for comfort, the answer may come in dismay, terror, and the turning aside of the Father's countenance because love itself will, for love's sake, turn the countenance away from that which is not lovely. And he will have to read, written on the dark wall of his imprisoned conscience, the words, awful and glorious, "Our God is a consuming fire."

Reflection

Why do you think God takes sin so seriously? Why is it that God cannot contradict His own character and laws?

16

The Eternal Truth of Christ

"I am the way, the truth, and the life.
No one comes to the Father except through Me."

JOHN 14:6

It may be many years before a man comes to see a truth—ages of strife, of effort, of aspiration. But once he does see it, it is so plain that he wonders how he could have lived without seeing it. That he did not understand it sooner was simply and only that he did not see it. To see a truth, to know what it is, to understand it, and to love it are all one. There is many a motion toward it, many a misery for want of it, many a cry of the conscience against the neglect of it, many a dim longing for it as an unknown need before at length the eyes come awake and the darkness of the dream-filled night yields to the light of the sun of truth. But once beheld, it is forever. To see one divine fact is to stand face-to-face with essential eternal life.

For this vision of truth God has been working for ages of ages. For this simple condition, this apex of life, upon which a man wonders like a child that he cannot make other men see as he sees, the whole labor of God's science, history, poetry—from the time when the earth gathered itself into a lonely drop of fire from the red rim of the driving sun-wheel. For this the patience of God will labor while there is yet a human soul whose eyes have not been opened, whose child-heart has not yet been born in him. For this one condition of humanity, this simple beholding, all the outthinking of God has flowed in forms innumerable and changeful from the foundation of the world.

Reflection

What keeps some of the people you know from seeing God's truth? How committed are you to knowing the truth of Christ and sharing it with other people who do not yet know Him?

God's Purifying Work

*"His winnowing fan is in His hand, and He will thoroughly
clean out His threshing floor, and gather His wheat into the barn;
but He will burn up the chaff with unquenchable fire."*

MATTHEW 3:12

It is the law of nature—that is, the law of God—that all that is destructible will be destroyed. When that which is immortal buries itself in the destructible, it cannot, though immortal still, know its own immortality. The destructible must be burned out of it, or begin to be burned out of it, before it can partake of eternal life. When that is all burned away and gone, it has eternal life. Or rather, when the fire of eternal life has possessed a man, the destructible is gone utterly, and he is pure.

Many a man's work must be burned, that by that very burning he may be saved—"so as by fire." Away in smoke go the lordships of the world, and the man who acquiesces in the burning is saved by the fire because it has destroyed the destructible, which would destroy both body and soul in hell. If he still clings to that which can be burned, the burning goes on deeper and deeper into his bosom until it reaches the roots of the falsehood that enslaves him—possibly by looking like the truth.

The man who loves God, and is not yet pure, courts the burning of God. The fire shows itself sometimes only as light—

still it will be fire of purifying. That which is not pure is cor-
ruptible, and corruption cannot inherit incorruption.

Reflection

In which area of your life do you need God's purifying fire?
Ask Him to help you, in His power, to face and overcome any
persistent sins in your life that lead to impurity.

18

Seek Community

———◦◦◦◦———

"If the whole body were an eye, where would be the hearing? If the whole were hearing, where would be the smelling? But now God has set the members, each one of them, in the body just as He pleased."

1 CORINTHIANS 12:17–18

We wrong those near us in being independent of them. We ought to lean on each other, giving and receiving—not as weaklings, but as lovers. Love is strength as well as need.

Reflection

Although being an independent person is often prized in our culture, why does such independence create weakness and disunity? How does, as the author asserts, being independent wrong those near us?

Living without God

*"The sons ... will be cast out into outer darkness.
There will be weeping and gnashing of teeth."*

MATTHEW 8:12

Even if a man thinks and cares little about God, he does not exist without God. God is here with him, upholding, warming, delighting, teaching him—making life a good thing to him. God gives him Himself, though he knows it not. But when God withdraws from a man as far as that can be without the man's ceasing to be; when the man himself feels abandoned, hanging in a ceaseless vertigo of existence upon the verge of the gulf of his being, without support, without refuge, without aim, without end, then will he listen in agony for the faintest sound of life from the closed door.

Then, if the moan of suffering humanity ever reaches the ear of the outcast of darkness, he will be ready to know life once more, to change this terror of sick negation, of unspeakable death, for that region of painful hope. Imagination cannot mislead us into too much horror of being without God—that one living death.

Reflection

Who, in your circle of influence, needs to hear the message of salvation? Why do we need to share, by word and deed, Jesus' message wherever we go?

Seek and You Will Find

"Ask, and it will be given to you; seek, and you will find; knock, and it will be opened to you."

MATTHEW 7:7

To the man who would live throughout the whole divine form of his being, not leaving the rest to the demons that haunt such deserts, a thousand questions will arise to which the Bible does not even allude. Do they lie beyond the sphere of his responsibility?

"No," replies the man. "Not only does that degree of peace of mind, without which action is impossible, depend on the answers to these questions, but my conduct itself must correspond to these answers."

Do we leave them at least until God chooses to explain?

"No. Questions imply answers. He has put the questions in my heart; He holds the answers in His. I will seek them from Him. I will wait, but not until I have knocked. I will be patient, but not until I have asked. I will seek until I find. He has something for me."

Reflection

What unanswered questions do you have for God? Are you asking Him to guide you to the answers, or have you kept your questions deeply buried?

Why Jesus Came to Earth

---

*"And the LORD, He is the One who goes before you. He will
be with you, He will not leave you nor forsake you;
do not fear nor be dismayed."*

DEUTERONOMY 31:8

Because we easily imagine ourselves in need, we imagine
that God is ready to forsake us. The miracles of Jesus were
the ordinary works of His Father, wrought small and swift that
we might take them in. The lesson of them was that help is
always within God's reach when His children want it.

The mission undertaken by the Son was not to show
Himself as having all power in heaven and earth, but to reveal
His Father, that men may know Him, and knowing, trust Him.
Jesus came to give them God, who is eternal life.

Reflection

Think about ways in which God has demonstrated His
faithfulness to you. Do you truly believe that He is willing to
help you? Will you trust Him fully?

The Holy Spirit's Revelation

"We all, with unveiled face, beholding as in a mirror
the glory of the Lord, are being transformed into the same image
from glory to glory, just as by the Spirit of the Lord."

2 CORINTHIANS 3:18

The great heresy of the church today is unbelief in the Holy Spirit. The majority of the church does not believe that the Spirit has a revelation for every person individually. The one use of the Bible is to make us look at Jesus, that through Him we might know His Father and our Father, His God and our God. Until we know Him, let us hold the Bible dear as the moon of our darkness, by which we travel toward the east.

A man will please God better by believing some things that are not told him than by confining his faith to those things that are expressly said—said to arouse in us the truth—seeing faculty, the spiritual desire, the prayer for the good things God will give to those who ask Him.

Some might protest, "Will not a man be taught thus to believe the things he likes best, even to pray for that which he likes best?" If it is true that the Spirit strives with our spirit and that God teaches men, we may safely leave the results to Him. If the man is of the Lord's company, he is safer with Him than with those who would secure their safety by hanging on the out-skirts and daring nothing. If he is not taught of God in that which he hopes for, God will let him know it. He will receive something other than he prays for. But it will be far better for him to be thus sharply tutored than to go on a snail's pace in the journey of the spiritual life.

Reflection

In what ways does the Holy Spirit reveal things to you? How can you tell what is the Spirit's revelation to you as opposed to your own inclinations and ideas?

23

Trust in God's Character

"O LORD my God, in You I put my trust."
PSALM 7:1

What should I think of my child if I found that he limited his faith in me and hope from me to the few promises he had heard me utter! The faith that limits itself to God's promises seems to me to partake of the paltry character of such a faith in my child—good enough for a pagan, but for a Christian a feeble faith. Those who rest in such a faith would feel even more comfortable if they had God's bond instead of His Word, which they regard not as the outcome of His character but as a pledge of His honor. They try to believe in the truth of His Word, but don't understand the truth of His being. Therefore, it is little wonder that they distrust those swellings of the heart that are His drawings of the man toward Him, as sun and moon heave the ocean mass heavenward.

Brother, sister, if such is your faith, you will not—must not—stop there. Come out of this bondage of the law to which you give the name of grace, for there is little that is gracious in it. You will yet know the dignity of your high calling and the love of God that passes knowledge. He is not afraid of your presumptuous approach to Him. It is you who are afraid to come near Him. He is not watching over His dignity. It is you who fear to be sent away as the disciples would have sent away the little children.

Our God, we will trust you. Will we not find you equal to our faith? One day, we will laugh ourselves to scorn that we looked for so little from you because your giving will not be limited by our hoping.

Reflection

Are you only trusting in God's promises—or in the full character of God? Why do you think God so deeply desires your faith and wants you to come boldly to Him? What may be keeping you from having stronger faith in Him?

Forgiveness Is Essential

*"If you forgive men their trespasses, your
heavenly Father will also forgive you."*

MATTHEW 6:14

He only is free whose love for another person is so strong that he can pardon the individual sin. He alone can pray the prayer, "Forgive us our trespasses," out of a full and genuine heart.

Forgiveness is the only cure for wrong. And hand in hand with "sense-of-injury" always walks the weak sister-demon "self-pity," so dear, so sweet to many. In short, forgiveness is freedom, forgiveness is liberation of the heart, mind, and soul.

Reflection

Is an area of unforgiveness lurking in your heart and mind? If so, confess it and forgive the person involved. Why do you think so many people don't want to offer forgiveness?

Time for a Change?

"He has made everything beautiful in its time."
ECCLESIASTES 3:11

Essential beauty is infinite. As the soul of Nature needs an endless succession of varied forms to embody her loveliness, countless faces of beauty springing forth, not any two the same, at every one of her heartthrobs, so the individual form needs an infinite change of its environments to enable it to uncover all the phases of its loveliness.

Sometimes change stimulates growth. Sometimes change prompts expansion into new areas. Sometimes change pushes and prods out of the old and into the new. Is it time for a change in your life?

Reflection

Why is it so easy to become stuck, to accept the status quo? What change is necessary to stimulate growth in your life?

26

Trust in God's Unfathomable Ways

―◦◦◦―

*"My thoughts are not your thoughts,
nor are your ways My ways,' says the LORD."*

ISAIAH 55:8

We know in whom we have believed, and we look for that which has not entered into the heart of man to conceive. Will God's thoughts be surpassed by man's thoughts? God's giving by man's asking? God's creation by man's imagination? No. Let us climb to the height of our Alpine desires; let us leave them behind us and ascend the spear-pointed Himalayas of our aspirations. Still will we find the depth of God's sapphire above us. Still will we find the heavens higher than the earth, and His thoughts and His ways higher than our thoughts and our ways.

Reflection

What happens in our lives when we try to make God think our thoughts and elevate our ways above His ways? How can you replace your thoughts with God's thoughts?

God's Powerful Words

*"Suddenly a voice came from heaven,
saying, 'This is My beloved Son, in whom I am well pleased.'"*

MATTHEW 3:17

The credibility of words depends upon their source—the person who speaks them. An utterance may seem commonplace until you are told that the one who spoke it is someone you admire and respect. Recognizing the mind from which the words proceed, you know the scale by which they are to be understood. So the words of God cannot mean just the same as the words of man.

"Can we not, then, understand them?" some may ask.

Yes, we can understand them—we can understand them more than the words of men. Whatever a good word means, as used by a good man, it means infinitely more as used by God. And the feeling or thought expressed by that word takes higher and higher forms in us as we become capable of understanding Him—that is, as we become like Him.

Reflection

How do we know when God is speaking to us? How has your understanding of God's Word grown the longer you have known Him as your Lord and Savior?

What God Thinks of You

*"To him who overcomes I will give some of the hidden manna to eat.
And I will give him a white stone, and on the stone a new name written
which no one knows except him who receives it."*

<small>REVELATION 2:17</small>

Each man has worth in God's sight. Life and action, thought
and intent are sacred. And what an end lies before us—
to have a consciousness of our own ideal being flashed into us
from the thought of God. Surely, for this may well give way
all our paltry self-consciousnesses, self-admirations, and self-
worships. Surely, to know what He thinks about us will push out
of our souls all our thoughts about ourselves. We may well hold
them loosely now, and be ready to let them go. Toward this
result St. Paul had already drawn near, when he who had begun
the race with a bitter cry for deliverance from the body of his
death was able to say that he judged his own self no longer.

Reflection

What is your perception of how God thinks of you? Why do
so many Christians have a distorted view of God's love and
acceptance of them?

The Hope of Being like Jesus

"Let us lay aside every weight, and the sin which so easily ensnares us, and let us run with endurance the race that is set before us, looking unto Jesus, the author and finisher of our faith."

HEBREWS 12:1–2

Demands unknown before are continually being made on the Christian. It is the ever-fresh rousing and calling, asking and sending of the Spirit that works in the children of obedience. When a person thinks he has arrived, then he is in danger. When the mountain he has so long been climbing suddenly shows a distant peak, a peak whose glory-crowned apex it seems as if no human foot could ever reach—then there is hope for him. There is then proof that he has been climbing, for he beholds the yet unclimbed. He sees what he could not see before. If he knows little of what he is, he knows something of what he is not. He learns ever afresh that he is not in the world as Jesus was in the world, but the very wind that breathes courage as he climbs is the hope that one day he will be like Jesus, seeing Him as He is.

Reflection

What challenges are you facing right now? Looking back over your spiritual life, in what ways have you grown? Ask the Holy Spirit to fill you with His presence as you seek to keep growing in your faith and better know Jesus.

Material Things Are Fleeting

---∞∞---

"We have this treasure in earthen vessels, that the
excellence of the power may be of God and not of us."

2 CORINTHIANS 4:7

It is not the fetters that *irritate* but the fetters that *soothe* that eat into the soul. When the fetters of gold on which the man delighted to gaze are gone, though they held him fast to his dungeon wall, buried from air and sunshine, then first will he feel them in the soreness of their lack, in the weary indifference with which he looks on earth and sea, on space and stars. When the truth begins to dawn on him that those fetters were a horror and a disgrace, then will man begin to understand that having never was, never could be well-being; that it is not by possessing we live, but by life we possess. It may seem to the man like the beginning of his slavery when it is in truth the beginning of his freedom. Never was a soul set free without being made to feel its slavery; nothing but itself can enslave a soul, nothing without itself free it.

But it is not the rich man only who is under the dominion of things. They, too, are slaves who, having no money, are unhappy from the lack of it. The man who is always digging his grave is little better than he who already lies moldering in it. The money the one has, the money the other would have, is in each the cause of an eternal stupidity.

Reflection

Where are you seeking contentment and freedom? How, in this culture, can you avoid becoming enslaved to material possessions?

Remember God's Care and Compassion

"'When I broke the five loaves for the five thousand, how many baskets full of fragments did you take up?' They said to Him, 'Twelve.' 'Also, when I broke the seven for the four thousand, how many large baskets full of fragments did you take up?' And they said, 'Seven.' So He said to them, 'How is it you do not understand?'"

MARK 8:19–21

After feeding the four thousand with seven loaves and a few small fishes, on the east side of the Sea of Galilee, Jesus, having crossed the lake, was met on the other side by certain Pharisees. Their attitude toward Him was such that He climbed back into the boat and recrossed the lake. On the way, the disciples thought they had in the boat but a single loaf. Probably while the Lord was occupied with the Pharisees, one of them had gone and bought it, little thinking they were about to start again so soon.

See how the disciples here fooled themselves! See how the Lord calls them to their senses. He doesn't tell them in so many words where they are wrong; He attacks instead the cause in themselves that led to their mistake—a matter always of infinitely more consequence than any mistake itself.

He reminds them of the two miracles with the loaves and the quantity of bread left beyond the need. From one of these miracles they had just come; it was not a day behind them. Yet here they were doubting already! He makes them go over the particulars of the miracle—but not to refresh their memories, for they were well aware of the marvel. He wants instead to make their hearts dwell on what they had already forgotten or had failed to see at all: the eternal fact of God's love, care, and compassion. They knew the number of the men each time, the number of the loaves each time, the number of the baskets of fragments they had each time picked up, but they forgot the Love that had so broken the bread that its remnants twenty times outweighed its loaves.

Reflection

When do you tend to focus on your problems rather than on God and His provision for you? Why, when we face deep challenges, is it important to remember what God has done for us in the past?

Reflecting on Winter and God's Plan

"While the earth remains, seedtime and harvest, cold and heat, winter and summer, and day and night shall not cease."

GENESIS 8:22

The winter drew on—a season as different from the summer in those northern latitudes as if it belonged to another solar system. Cold and stormy, it is yet full of delight for all beings who can either romp, sleep, or think it through.

One morning, all the children awoke and saw a white world around them. It was a sunny, frosty morning. The snow had fallen all night, with its own silence, and no wind had interfered with the gracious alightings of the feathery water. Every branch, every twig, was laden with its sparkling burden of down-flickered flakes and threw long lovely shadows on the smooth featureless dazzle below. Away, away stretched the outspread glory, the only darkness in it being the line of the winding river. All the snow that fell on it vanished, as death and hell will one day vanish in the fire of God. It flowed on, black through its banks of white. Away again stretched the shine to the town, where every roof had the sheet that was let down from heaven spread over it, and the streets lay a foot deep in yet unsullied snow, soon, like the story of the ages, to be trampled, soiled, wrought, and driven with human feet until, at last, God's strong sun would wipe it all away.

Reflection

Are your senses in tune with the glorious seasons of nature God has provided? In what ways do the changing seasons reflect God's character and creativity?

Yield Yourself to God's Workmanship

"Present ... your members as instruments of righteousness to God."
ROMANS 6:13

He who fancies himself the carver finds himself but the chisel, or indeed perhaps only the mallet, in the hand of the true Workman.

Reflection

Have you fully yielded yourself to God? Do you ask Him to use you—your skills, your resources, your entire self—in whatever way He chooses? What kinds of things happen when someone tries to be the "carver" and ignores God?

Facing the Truth of Christ

"When He, the Spirit of truth, has come, He will guide you into all truth."
JOHN 16:13

Whatever belongs to the region of thought and feeling, and uttered in words, is of necessity uttered imperfectly. Thought and feeling are infinite, and human speech, although far-reaching in scope and marvelous in delicacy, can embody them but approximately and imprecisely.

Our Lord had no design of constructing a system of truth in intellectual forms. He spoke the truth of the moment in its relation to Himself. He spoke out of a region of realities that He knew could only be suggested—not represented—in the forms of intellect and speech. With vivid flashes of life and truth, His words invade our darkness, rousing us with sharp stings of light to will our awaking, to arise from the dead and cry for the light that He can give, not in the lightning of words only, but in indwelling presence and power.

Better to refuse even the truth for a time than, not seeing its real form, to introduce hesitation into our prayers, a discordant sound into our praises, and a misery into our love. If it is the truth, we will one day see it as another thing than it appears now.

Let us endeavor to follow Jesus wholeheartedly and, within our limited capabilities, listen for His truth. Even when we cannot comprehend it, we can trust Him who *is* Truth.

Reflection

How can we discern true spiritual truth? What role does the Holy Spirit play in teaching us?

The Path of God's Forgiveness

*"You, LORD, are good, and ready to forgive, and
abundant in mercy to all those who call upon You."*

PSALM 86:5

There are various kinds and degrees of wrongdoing, which
need varying kinds and degrees of forgiveness. An out-
burst of anger in a child, for instance, scarcely requires
forgiveness. The wrong in it may be so small that the parent has
only to emphasize for the child the need for self-restraint and
patience. The father will not feel that such a fault has built up
any wall between him and his child. But suppose that he discovered in the child a habit of sly cruelty toward his younger
brothers or the animals of the house? How differently would he
feel! Could his response be the same as in the former case?
Would not the different transgression require a different form
of forgiveness? Would not the forgiveness have to take the form
of that kind of punishment best fit for correction? Could there
be true love in any other kind of forgiveness than this?

God is forgiving us every day—blowing away the fog,
caused by sin, that obscures our view of Him. When sin has
clouded our horizon and hidden Him from our eyes, He sweeps
away a path for His forgiveness to reach our hearts, that it may
by causing our repentance destroy the wrong and even make us
able to forgive ourselves. For some are too proud to forgive
themselves until God's forgiveness has had its way with them,

has drowned their pride in tears of repentance, and made their heart again like the heart of a little child.

Reflection

In what ways does our sin and God's appropriate response teach us valuable lessons? Why is it sometimes difficult to forgive ourselves, even though God eagerly and completely forgives?

When Troubles Arise, Appeal to God

"Humble yourselves under the mighty hand of God, that He may exalt you in due time, casting all your care upon Him, for He cares for you."

1 PETER 5:6–7

With every haunting trouble, great or small, go to God and appeal to Him. For He is the God of your life, ready to deliver you. If your trouble is such that you feel you cannot appeal to Him, the more need you have to appeal to Him! When one cannot go to God, there is something especially wrong.

If you let thoughts about tomorrow, or the next month, or the next year distress you; if you let rumors and gossip annoy you; if you seek or greatly heed the judgment of men, capable or incapable, you open your windows to the mosquitoes of care, to drown out with their buzzing the voice of the eternal! In all things, seek the comfort and healing of God.

Reflection

Do you *really* believe that God cares about even your smallest troubles and act on that belief? Think about His faithfulness, and make a special effort to bring even small anxieties to Him.

God Hates Pride

―――∘≪≫∘―――

*"For from within, out of the heart of men,
proceed evil thoughts, adulteries ... pride."*

MARK 7:21–22

Ambition in every shape has to do with things, with outward advantages for the satisfaction of self-worship. It is that form of pride, foul shadow of Satan, that usurps the place of aspiration. The sole ambition that is of God is the ambition to rise above oneself; all other is of the Devil. Yet it is nursed and cherished in many a soul who thinks itself devout, filling it with petty cares and disappointments that swarm like bats in its air and shut out the glory of God.

The love of the praise of men, the desire for fame, the pride that takes offense, the puffing-up of knowledge—these and every other form of self-worship—we must get rid of them all. To him who considers himself higher than he truly is, who has not humbled himself as a servant, God will not enter in; He will not dine with him (Rev. 3:20). The Father desires to sit by the humblest hearth, where the daily food is prepared in simplicity and meekness.

Reflection

Why is pride so dangerous—and also so hard to root out of our lives? What keeps God from blessing proud, self-seeking people? In what ways is pride affecting Christians around you?

Pray with Persistence

"He spoke a parable to them, that men always ought to pray and not lose heart…. 'Now there was a widow in that city; and she came to him [a judge], saying, "Get justice for me from my adversary." And he would not for a while; but afterward he said within himself, "Though I do not fear God nor regard man, yet because this widow troubles me I will avenge her."'"

LUKE 18:1, 3–5

It is a comfort that the Lord sees we need encouragement to go on praying, that it looks as if we were not heard, that it is no wonder we should be ready to give up. He tells a parable in which the supplicant has to go often to the man who can help her, receiving help only at long last.

Here, as elsewhere, Jesus teaches us that we must not go by the look of things, but by the reality behind the look. A truth, a necessity of God's own willed nature, is enough to set up against a whole army of appearances. It looks as if He does not hear you; never mind, He does. It must be that He does. Persist as did the woman in the parable; you, too, will be heard. She is heard at last, in response to her perseverance; God hears at once and will avenge speedily (Luke 18:8).

The unrighteous judge cared nothing for the woman, but those who cry to God are His own chosen—illustrated in the fact that they cry to Him. He has made and appointed them to cry: they do cry. Will He not hear them? They exist that they may pray. He has chosen them that they may choose Him. He has called them that they may call Him. In doing so, there will be deep communion, as belongs to a Father and His child.

Reflection

How persistent are you in your prayer life? Why do you think Jesus told this parable? What happens if we "go by the look of things" rather than by the truth of God's character?

39

Tempted by Good

———◦◦◦◦◦———

"Then Jesus was led up by the Spirit into the
wilderness to be tempted by the devil."

MATTHEW 4:1

If anyone says that Jesus was not moved by those temptations, that person must also believe that they weren't genuine temptations at all. Nor, in that case, was His victory of more significance than that of the man who, tempted to bear false witness against his neighbor, abstains from robbing him of his goods. Regarding human need, struggle, and hope, it bears no meaning, and we must reject the whole as a fantastic folly of crude invention—a mere stage show, a lie for the poor sake of the fancied truth.

So how could He then be the Son of His Father, who cannot be tempted with evil? In the answer to this lies the center, the essential germ of the whole interpretation. He was not tempted with evil but with good—with inferior forms of good, that is, pressing in on Him while higher forms of good held themselves aloof. I do not believe the Son of God could be tempted with evil, but I believe that He could be tempted with good—to yield to whichever temptation would have been evil in Him, bringing ruin to the universe.

But doesn't all evil come from good? Yes, but a good corrupted is no longer a good. Evil is evil whatever it may have come from. The Lord could not have felt tempted to take vengeance on His enemies, but He might have felt tempted to destroy the wicked from the face of the earth.

Reflection

What new light does this reading shed on the temptations of Jesus? In today's culture, what are some examples of good things that may tempt us to do evil?

Hold Fast to Your Hopes

*"According to His abundant mercy [God] has begotten us
again to a living hope through the resurrection of Jesus Christ
from the dead, to an inheritance incorruptible and undefiled
and that does not fade away, reserved in heaven for you."*

1 PETER 1:3–4

The best preparation for a disappointment is the hope that precedes it. Let us hold fast by our hopes. All colors are shreds of the rainbow. There is a rainbow of the cataract, of the paddle wheel, of the falling wave. None is the rainbow, yet they are all of it. All vanish, but that which set them in their places and will set them again—the rainbow in the heart of God— never vanishes. Say not that they are but hopes because by our hopes we are saved. It is because they are not the thing hoped for that they are precious, because the thing itself would block the way of a higher gift for which the deeper nature is longing through and beyond the hope, and includes the object of it.

The rainbow is the color palette light created by the dark teardrops of the world. Hope is the shimmer on the web of history, whose warp of trouble is shot with the woof of God's intent.

Reflection

In what or whom have you placed your hopes? Pause to reflect on the hope every believer has through what Jesus accomplished by the cross and His resurrection.

Jesus, the Precious Word

*"In the beginning was the Word, and the Word was
with God, and the Word was God."*

JOHN 1:1

To understand the words of our Lord is the business of life,
because it is the main road to the understanding of The
Word Himself. And to receive Him is to receive the Father, and
so to have Life in ourselves. And Life—the higher, the deeper,
the simpler—is the business of life.

The Word is that by which we live, namely, Jesus Himself,
and His words represent, in part, in shadow, in suggestion,
Himself. Any utterance worthy of being called a truth is human
food. The Son came forth to be, before our eyes and in our
hearts, that which He had made us for, that we might behold
the truth in Him and cry out for the living God, who, in the
highest sense of all is The Truth. The Lord said, "I am ... the
truth" (John 14:6), and by those who are in some measure like
Him in being the truth, The Word can be understood. Let us
try to understand Him.

Sometimes, no doubt, the Savior would have used a different fashion of speech if he had come to Englishmen instead of
to Jews. But the lessons He gave would have been the same.
Even when questioned about a matter for its passing import,
His reply contained the enunciation of the great human princi-
ple that lay in it. His every response lies changeless in every

variation of changeful circumstance. With the light of added ages of Christian experience, it ought to be easier for us to understand His words than it was for those who heard Him.

Reflection

How eager are you to understand the truths of Jesus, and to share them with other people in your sphere of influence? Why, in our culture today, is the Bible's absolute truth so important?

The Heart of the Matter

*"Do not lay up for yourselves treasures on earth, where moth
and rust destroy and where thieves break in and steal;
but lay up for yourselves treasures in heaven, where neither
moth nor rust destroys and where thieves do not break in and steal.
For where your treasure is, there your heart will be also."*

MATTHEW 6:19–21

What is with the treasure must fare as the treasure; the heart that haunts the treasure house where moth and rust corrupt will be exposed to the same ravages as the treasure, will itself be rusted and moth-eaten. Many a man and a woman, fair and flourishing to see, has a rusty, moth-eaten heart within that form of strength or beauty.

"But this is only a figure of speech," some would argue.

True. But is the reality intended less or more than the figure? Doesn't the rust and moth mean more than disease? Doesn't the heart mean more than the heart? Doesn't it mean a deeper heart, the heart of your own self, not of your body? A heart that is the innermost chamber wherein springs the divine fountain of your being? A heart God regards, though you may never have known its existence, not even when its writhings under the gnawing of the moth and the slow fire of the rust have communicated a dull pain to that outer heart that sends the blood?

If God sees that heart corroded with the rust of cares, riddled into caverns by worms of ambition and greed, your heart is as God sees it because He sees things as they are.

One day you will be compelled to see—no, to feel—your heart as God sees it. You will know that the corrupted thing within you, a prey to the vilest of diseases, is indeed the center of your being, your very heart.

Reflection

What kind of shape is your innermost *heart* really in? Which treasures do you seek? Where is your heart?

The Perils of Compromise

"No one can serve two masters.... You cannot serve God and mammon."
MATTHEW 6:24

To the man born to riches, they seem not merely a natural but an essential condition of well-being, and the man who has made his money feels that it is his by the labor of his soul, the travail of the day, and the care of the night. Each person feels a right to have and to hold the things he possesses. If there is a necessity for his entering into the kingdom of heaven, it is hard indeed that right and necessity should confront each other and constitute all but a bare impossibility! Why should he not "make the best of both worlds"? He would compromise, if he might; he would serve mammon a little and God much. He would not have such a "best of both worlds" that comes by putting the lower in utter subservience to the higher—of casting away the treasure of this world and taking the treasure of heaven instead. He would gain as little as may be of heaven—but something, with the loss of as little as possible of the world. That which he desires of heaven is not its best; that which he would not yield of the world is its most worthless.

Reflection

Why can't a person "serve" God and money at the same time? What pressures to compromise do you face in regard to money?

44

Why Forgive?

"Forgive, and you will be forgiven."
LUKE 6:37

When we forgive our neighbor, in flows the consciousness of God's forgiveness to us. In the act of forgiving, we become capable of believing that God can forgive us. Conversely, no man who will not forgive his neighbor can believe that God is willing to forgive him.

If God said "I forgive you" to a man who hated his brother, and if (as is impossible) that voice of forgiveness should reach the man, what would it mean to him? How would the man interpret it? Would it not mean to him, "You may go on hating. I do not mind it. You have had great provocation and are justified in your hate"? The man would think, not that God loved the sinner, but that He overlooked the sin, which God never does. While a man continues in such a mood, God cannot be with him as his friend; not that He will not be his friend, but the friendship being all on one side—that of God—must take forms such as the man will not be able to recognize as friendship. Forgiveness is not love merely, but love conveyed as love to the erring, so establishing peace toward God and forgiveness toward our neighbor.

Reflection

Why is it important for each of us to think about forgiveness and its impact on other people, God, and ourselves? Which people have forgiven you? How did you feel afterward?

Pursue the True, Narrow Way

"Enter by the narrow gate."

MATTHEW 7:13

The narrow ways trodden by men are miserable; they have high walls on each side and only an occasional glimpse of the sky above. The true way, though narrow, is not unlovely; most footpaths are lovelier than high roads. It may be full of toil, but it cannot be miserable. It has not walls, but fields and forests and gardens around it, and limitless sky overhead. It has its sorrows, but many of them lie only on its borders, and those people who leave the path gather them.

Reflection

What are some of the differences found on God's true, narrow path and the world's path? If you tread the paths on which God would have you walk, what beauty have you discovered along the way?

A Prayer about Experiencing God

"Walk humbly with your God."
MICAH 6:8

This day be with me, Lord, when I go forth,
  Be nearer to me than I am able to ask.
In merriment, in conversation, or in task,
Walking the street, listening to men of worth,
Or greeting such as only talk and bask,
Be thy thought still my waiting soul around,
And if He come, I shall be watching found.

Be with me, Lord. Keep me beyond all prayers:
For more than all my prayers my need of Thee,
And Thou beyond all need, all unknown cares;
What the heart's dear imagination dares,
Thou dost transcend in measureless majesty.
All prayers in one—my God, be unto me
Thy own eternal self, absolutely.

Reflection

How deeply do you desire to know God and feel His presence? Why must you pursue God's presence every day?

Do You Fill Time or Kill Time?

"A wise man's heart discerns both time and judgment, because for every matter there is a time and judgment, though the misery of man increases greatly. For he does not know what will happen."

ECCLESIASTES 8:5–7

Waiting patiently and with a pure heart is perhaps the hardest thing for flesh and blood to do well. The relations of time to mind are very strange. Some of their phenomena seem to prove that time is only of the mind—belonging to the intellect, as good and evil belong to the spirit. Anyhow, if it were not for the clocks of the universe, one man would live a year or a century where another would live but a day. But the mere notion of time, not to say the consciousness of *empty* time, is fearful. It is this empty time that the fool is always trying to kill; his effort should be to fill it. Yet nothing but the living God can fill it—though it be but the shape our existence takes to it. Only where He is, emptiness is not. Eternity will be but an intense present to the child with whom is the Father.

Reflection

What does it means to "fill time" rather than "kill time"? What did the author mean when he wrote that "nothing but the living God can fill" time?

The First Temptation of Christ

"When the tempter came to Him, he said, 'If You are the Son of God, command that these stones become bread.'"

MATTHEW 4:3

The Lord had been fasting for forty days—a fast impossible except during intense mental absorption. Let no one think to glorify this fast by calling it miraculous. Such fasts are on record on the part of holy men. Inasmuch as the Lord was more of a man than His brethren, He might have been farther withdrawn in the depths of His spiritual humanity from the outer region of His physical nature. Fasting in His case might thus be extended beyond the utmost limits of similar fasts in others.

What a temptation was here! There is no sin in wishing to eat, no sin in procuring food honestly that one find sustenance. But it rises even into an awful duty when a man knows that to eat will restore the lost vision of the eternal. To eat would render the man capable of hope as well as faith, of gladness as well as confidence, of praise as well as patience. Why then should He not eat? Why should He not put forth the power that was in Him that He might eat? Because such power was His, not to take care of Himself but to perform the work of the Father who sent Him. Because it was God's business to take care of Him, His to do what the Father told Him to do. To make that stone bread would be to take the care out of the Father's hands and

turn the divinest thing in the universe into the merest commonplace of self-preservation.

Reflection

Why are we often tempted to try to take care of ourselves
rather than trusting God to care for us? Think about any areas
of life in which you are more focused on caring for yourself
than doing the work of God.

The Second Temptation of Christ

"Then the devil took Him up into the holy city, set Him on the pinnacle of the temple, and said to Him, 'If You are the Son of God, throw Yourself down. For it is written: "He shall give His angels charge over you."'"

MATTHEW 4:5–6

Satan quotes Scripture as a verbal authority; our Lord meets him with a Scripture by the truth in which He regulates His conduct. If we examine it, we will find that to the Son of God, the will of God is Life. It was a temptation to show the world's powers that He was the Son of God, that to Him the elements were subject, that He was above the laws of nature because He was the eternal Son, and thus stop the raging of the heathen and people's vain imaginations. It would be but to show them the truth.

But He was the Son of God; what was His Father's will? This was not the divine way of convincing the world of sin, righteousness, and judgment. If the Father told Him to cast Himself down, that moment the pinnacle pointed naked to the sky. If the Devil threw Him down, let God send His angels or, if better, allow Him to be dashed to pieces in the valley below. But never will He forestall the divine will. The Father will order what comes next. The Son will obey.

In the path of His work, Christ will turn aside for no stone. There let the angels bear Him in their hands if need be. But He will not choose the path because there is a stone in it. He will not choose at all. He will go where the Spirit leads Him.

The truth must show itself in God's time, in and by the labor. The kingdom must come in God's holy, human way. Not by a stroke of grandeur, but by years of love, yea, by centuries of seeming bafflement, by eons of labor, must He grow into the hearts of the sons and daughters of His Father in heaven.

Reflection

Why is it so important to be sensitive to God's leading rather than just acting on what we think? How do we reconcile taking action with obeying God in accordance with His will?

Nothing But the Truth

"The truthful lip shall be established forever.... Lying lips are an abomination to the LORD, but those who deal truthfully are His delight."

PROVERBS 12:19, 22

R eal approximation, real union, must ever be in proportion to mutual truthfulness.

Reflection

Do you find it easy to be truthful in *all* areas of your life? How might even the most secret deceit be affecting your relationship with God? With other people?

Victory over Physical Death

"Do not be afraid, for I know that you seek
Jesus who was crucified. He is not here; for He is risen."

MATTHEW 28:5–6

Come here, Malcolm," said Mr. Graham, and took him by the arm and led him toward the east end of the church, where a few tombstones were crowded against the wall, as if they would press close to a place they might not enter.

"Read that," he said, pointing to a flat stone, where every hollow letter was shown in high relief by the growth in it of a lovely moss. The rest of the stone was rich in gray and green and brown lichens, but only in the letters grew the bright moss. The inscription stood as it were in the hand of Nature herself: "He is not here; for He is risen."

While Malcolm gazed, trying to think what his master would have him think, the latter resumed. "If He is risen—if the sun is up, Malcolm—then the morning and not the evening is the season for the place of tombs; the morning when the shadows are shortening and separating, not the evening when they are growing all into one. I used to love the churchyard best in the evening, when the past was more to me than the future; now I visit it almost every bright summer morning, and only occasionally at night."

"But, sir, isna deith a dreidfu' thing?" said Malcolm.

"That depends on whether a man regards it as his fate, or

as the will of a perfect God. Its obscurity is its dread. But if God be light, then death itself must be full of splendor—a splendor probably too keen for our eyes to receive."

Reflection

How do you view physical death? What light does God's Word shed on your eternal future in heaven? On what heaven will be like?

52

Share the
Great Truths of God

―――◦◦◦◦∘―――

*"God our Savior ... desires all men to be saved
and to come to the knowledge of the truth."*

1 Timothy 2:3–4

I can understand how a man might live, like the good hermits of old, in continual meditation upon all-satisfying truths, and let the waves of the world's time wash by him in unheeded flow until his cell changed to his tomb and his spirit soared free. But to spend your time in giving little lessons when you have great ones to give; in enforcing the old law, "You shall love your neighbor as yourself," when you know in your own heart that not a person can ever learn to keep it without first learning to fulfill an infinitely greater one—to love his neighbor even as Christ has loved him—then indeed one may well grow disheartened and feel as if he were not in the place prepared for, and at the work required of, him.

Reflection

Why is it sometimes easy to become trapped in sharing small spiritual truths when God is calling us to share much larger truths about Himself? What are some of the "greater" truths we are focus on and share with others?

Obeying the Father's Will

*"Jesus said to Peter, 'Put your sword into the sheath.
Shall I not drink the cup which My Father has given Me?'"*

JOHN 18:11

Nothing but the Son's obedience, the obedience to the death, the absolute doing of the Father's will, could redeem the prisoner, widow, and orphan. But it would redeem them by redeeming the conquest-ridden conqueror, too, the stripe-giving jailer, the unjust judge, the petty and conniving Pharisee. The earth would be free because love was stronger than death. Therefore should fierceness, wrong, hypocrisy, and God-service play out their weary play, Jesus would not pluck the spreading branches of the tree. He would lay the ax to its root. It would take time, but the tree would be dead at last— dead and cast into the lake of fire. It would take time; but His Father had time enough and to spare. It would take courage, strength, self-denial, and endurance, but His Father could give Him all. It would cost agony of body and mind, but those He was ready to take on Himself.

It would cost Him the vision of many sad and, to all but Him, hopeless sights. He must see tears without wiping them, hear sighs without changing them into laughter, see the dead lie and let them lie, see Rachel weeping for her children and refusing to be comforted. He must look on His brothers and sisters crying as children over their broken toys and must not mend them. He must go on to the grave, and they not know that thus He was setting all things right for them. His work must be one with and completing God's creation and God's history. The disappointment, sorrow, and fear He could, He would bear. The will of God would be done. Man would be free—not merely man as he thinks of himself, but man as God thinks of him. The divine idea would be set free in the divine bosom; God's great, beautiful, and perfect will must be done.

Reflection

What aspects of Jesus' commitment to doing the will of His Father apply to your life today? How committed are you to pursuing God's will above all else, no matter what the sacrifice may be?

The Source of All Goodness

"Oh, give thanks to the LORD, for He is good!"
PSALM 106:1

There is one living good, in whom the good thing, and all good, is alive and ever operative. Ask me not about the good thing, but the good person, the good being—the origin of all "good"—who, because He is, can make good. He is ready with His life to communicate living good, and so doing good, for He makes good itself to exist. It is not with this good thing and that good thing we have to do, but with that power from which comes our power even to speak the word *good*.

To look upon God is to recognize our need for His goodness; to think about Him is to begin to be good. It is not to make us do all things right He cares about, but to make us hunger and thirst after righteousness. In pursuing righteousness, we will never need to think of what is or is not good, but will refuse the evil and choose the good out of inclination and inspiration of the heart.

Reflection

What's the relationship between goodness and knowing God? Where do we get the strength of will to stand for good and refuse evil?

A Most Important Choice

*"Jesus said to him, 'If you want to be perfect, go,
sell what you have and give to the poor, and you will
have treasure in heaven; and come, follow Me.'"*

MATTHEW 19:21

Having kept the commandments, the youth needed and was ready for a further lesson. The Lord would not leave him where he was; He had come to seek and to save. He saw him in need of perfection—the thing the commonplace Christian thinks he can best do without.

To gain the perfection the young man desired, the one thing lacking was that he should sell all he had, give it to the poor, and follow the Lord. Could this be all that lay between him and entering into life? God only knows what the victory of such obedience might at once have wrought in him! As things were, he was a slave because a man is in bondage to whatever he cannot part with. Jesus could have taken his possessions from him by an exercise of His will, but there would have been little good in that; He wished to do it by the exercise of the young man's will. That would be a victory indeed for both. So would he enter into freedom and life, delivered from mammon's bondage by the Lord's lovely will in him, one with his own.

The young man would not do what was necessary. It was possible for him to respond, to give birth, by obedience, to the redeemed and redeeming will, and so be free. It was time the demand should be made on him. Do you say, "But he would not respond, he would not obey!"? Then it was time, I answer, that he should refuse, that he should know what manner of spirit he was of and meet the confusions of soul, the sad searchings of heart that must follow. A time comes to every man when he must obey or make such refusal—and know it.

Reflection

To what degree are you a "slave" to possessions—or anything else? What might God want you to give up so that you can obey Him more fully?

God Lifts Us Up

*"Show me Your ways, O LORD; teach me
Your paths. Lead me in Your truth and teach me,
for You are the God of my salvation."*

PSALM 25:4–5

Whatever it is that keeps the finer faculties of the mind awake, wonder alive, and the interest above mere eating and drinking, moneymaking and money saving; whatever it is that gives gladness, sorrow, or hope is simply a divine gift that comes with salvation. It is the gift of life, through Jesus Christ, that lifts us out of the mire and up on the rock. It keeps a way open for the entrance of deeper, holier, grander influences emanating from the same riches of the Godhead.

Reflection

Which activities in your life draw you closer to God and His amazing blessings? If you are not doing them regularly, how might you invite them back into your daily life?

Christ's Faith in the Midst of Suffering

*"He was wounded for our transgressions, He was bruised for
our iniquities; the chastisement for our peace was
upon Him, and by His stripes we are healed."*

ISAIAH 53:5

We should approach the terrible fact of our Lord's sufferings with the holiest fear. Let no one think that those were less because He was more. The more delicate the nature, the more alive to all that is lovely, true, lawful, and right.

Christ's sufferings were awful indeed when they began to invade the region about the will—when the struggle to keep consciously trusting in God began to sink in darkness, when the will of the Man put forth its last determined effort in that cry after the vanishing vision of the Father: "My God, My God, why have You forsaken Me?" (Mark 15:34). Thus Jesus' will, in the very moment when His faith seems about to yield, is finally triumphant. It has no feeling now to support it, no beatific vision to absorb it. It stands naked in His soul and tortured, as He stood naked and scourged before Pilate. Pure, simple, and surrounded by fire, it declares for God. The sacrifice ascends in the cry, "My God." The cry comes not out of happiness, peace, hope. Not even out of suffering comes that cry. It was a cry in desolation, but it came out of faith. It is the last voice of Truth, speaking when it can but cry. The divine horror of that moment is unfathomable by human soul. It was blackness. Yet He would believe. Yet He would hold fast. God was still His God. "My God"—in the cry came forth the victory, and all was over soon. Of the peace that followed that cry, the peace of a perfect soul, large as the universe, pure as light, ardent as life, victorious for God and His brethren, He alone can ever know the breadth, length, depth, and height.

Reflection

Think about the sacrifice Jesus made for you, and how faithful He was in going to the cross. Are you holding fast to Him even when times are terribly difficult?

Reeds Blown by the Wind

"Choose for yourselves this day whom you will serve."

JOSHUA 24:15

As long as we have nothing to say to God, nothing to do with Him except in the sunshine of the mind when we feel Him near us, we are poor creatures, willed upon, not willing. We are like reeds, perhaps flowering and pleasant to behold, but only reeds blown about by the wind. Not bad, but poor creatures.

And how in such a condition do we generally act? Don't we sit mourning over the loss of our feelings? Or worse, make frantic efforts to rouse them? Or, ten times worse, relapse into a state of temporary atheism and yield to the pressing temptation? Or, being heartless, consent to remain careless, conscious of evil thoughts and low feelings alone, but too lazy, too content to rouse ourselves against them? We know we must get rid of them someday, but meanwhile—never mind; we do not feel them bad, we do not feel anything else good. We are asleep, and we know it, and we cannot be troubled to wake. No impulse comes to arouse us, so we remain as we are.

God doesn't make us always feel right, desire good, love purity, and aspire after Him and His will. The truth is this: He wants to make us in His own image, choosing the good, refusing the evil. How could He accomplish this if He were always moving us from within, as He does at divine intervals, toward the beauty of holiness?

Reflection

Why does God want you to *choose* to obey Him and turn from evil? Which things tempt you to "let things slide" and to put off pursuing holiness?

The Mystery of Free Will

"I have set before you life and death, blessing and cursing; therefore choose life, that both you and your descendants may live; that you may love the LORD your God, that you may obey His voice, and that you may cling to Him, for He is your life and the length of your days."

DEUTERONOMY 30:19–20

God gives us room to be and doesn't oppress us with His will. He "stands away from us" that we may act from ourselves, that we may exercise the pure will for good. Do not, therefore, imagine me to mean that we can do anything of ourselves without God. If we choose the right at last, it is all God's doing, and only the more His that it is ours, only in a far more marvelous way His than if He had kept us filled with all holy impulses precluding the need of choice.

Up to this very point, for this very point, He has been educating us, leading us, pushing us, driving us, enticing us, that we may choose Him and His will—and so be tenfold more His children, of His own best making. God made our individuality as well as, and a greater marvel than, our dependence; made our apartness from Himself, that freedom should bind us divinely dearer to Himself, with a new and inscrutable marvel of love. The Godhead is still at the root, is the making root of our individuality. The freer the man, the stronger the bond that binds him to Him who made his freedom. God made our wills and is striving to make them free, for only in the perfection of our individuality and the freedom of our wills can we be altogether His children. This is full of mystery, but can we not see enough in it to make us very glad and peaceful?

Reflection

Why does God give each person free will and ability to make choices? What do your choices reveal about your commitment to God and His will?

Faith during Challenging Times

"Thomas answered and said to Him, 'My Lord and my God!'"
JOHN 20:28

When the inward sun is shining, and the wind of thought, blowing amidst the flowers and leaves of fancy and imagination, rouses glad forms and feelings, it is easy to look upward and say, "My God." It is easy when the frosts of external failure have braced the mental nerves to healthy endurance and fresh effort after labor. It is easy then to turn to God and trust in Him, in whom all honest exertion gives an ability as well as a right to trust. It is easy in pain, as long as it does not pass certain undefinable boundaries, to hope in God for deliverance or pray for strength to endure.

But what is to be done when all feeling is gone? When a man doesn't know whether he believes or not, whether he loves or not? When art, poetry, and religion are nothing to him, so swallowed up is he in pain, mental depression, disappointment, temptation, or he knows not what? It seems to him then that God doesn't care for him, and certainly he does not care for God. If he is still humble, he thinks that he is so bad that God cannot care for him. And he then believes for the time that God loves us only because and when and while we love Him—instead of believing that God loves us always because He is our God and we live only by His love. Or he does not believe in a God at all, which is better.

Reflection

How have you responded to God during difficult situations—when you feel you can't take any more pain, doubt, rejection, frustration, temptation, or depression? What did you think about the last sentence of this reading?

Drawn toward God

"I will lift up my eyes to the hills—from whence comes my help?
My help comes from the LORD, who made heaven and earth."

PSALM 121:1–2

Some people will endure an immense amount of misery before they feel compelled to look for help, from where all help and healing comes. They cannot believe that there is truly an unseen mysterious power, until the world and all that is in it has vanished in the smoke of despair; until cause and effect is nothing to the intellect, and possible glories have faded from the imagination. Then, deprived of all that made life pleasant or hopeful, the immortal essence, lonely and wretched and unable to cease, looks up with its now unfettered and wakened intellect to the source of its own life—to the possible God who, notwithstanding all the improbabilities of His existence, may yet perhaps be, and may yet perhaps hear His wretched creature who calls.

In this loneliness of despair, life must find The Life; for joy is gone, and life is all that is left. It is compelled to seek its source, its roots, its eternal life. This alone remains as a possible thing. Other simpler natures look up at once. Even before the first pang has passed away, as by a holy instinct of celestial childhood, they lift their eyes to the heavens from whence their help comes.

Reflection

Is anything keeping you from truly seeking God and His blessings? How might God use what you have learned through suffering to help other people who are on the journey toward faith in Him?

A Prayer for God's Presence

"Our soul waits for the LORD; He is our help and our shield. For our heart shall rejoice in Him, because we have trusted in His holy name."

PSALM 33:20–21

B e Thou the well by which I lie and rest;
Be Thou my tree of life, my garden ground;
Be Thou my home, my fire, my chamber blessed,
My book of wisdom, loved of all the best;
Oh, be my friend, each day still newer found,
As the eternal days and nights go round!
Nay, nay—You are *my God*, in whom all loves are bound!

Reflection

What does it mean, specifically, to have God present with you? When was the last time you clearly felt God's presence in your life?

Conformed to the Image of God

---

*"The Lord talked with you face to face on the mountain from
the midst of the fire. I stood between the Lord and you at that
time, to declare to you the word of the Lord; for you were afraid
because of the fire, and you did not go up the mountain."*

Deuteronomy 5:4–5

Here was a nation at its lowest. Could it receive anything
but a partial revelation, a revelation of fear? How should
the Hebrews be other than terrified at that which was opposed
to all they knew of themselves, who judged it good to honor a
golden calf? Such as they were, they did well to be afraid. They
were in a better condition, acknowledging if only a terror above
them, flaming on that unknown mountain height, than stoop-
ing to worship the idol below them.

Fear is nobler than sensuality. Fear is better than no God,
better than a god made with hands. In that fear lay deeply hidden the sense of the infinite. The worship of fear is true,
although very low. Although not acceptable to God in itself, for
only the worship of spirit and of truth is acceptable to Him, yet
even in His sight it is precious. For He regards men not as they
are merely, but as they will be; not as they will be merely, but
as they are now growing, or capable of growing, toward that
image after which He made them that they might grow to it.
Therefore, a thousand stages, each in itself all but valueless, are

of inestimable worth as the necessary and connected grada-
tions of an infinite progress.

Reflection

Although the ancient Israelites were afraid of God and His
holy fire, they were also growing spiritually, slowly, and gradu-
ally. What happens when we expect brand-new Christians to
take huge bounds toward God rather than being patient with
their "baby steps"? How does God view our progress, slow as it
may be, toward becoming more like Him?

Faith beyond Feelings

"They cried out to the LORD in their trouble, and He saved them out of their distresses. He brought them out of darkness and the shadow of death, and broke their chains in pieces."

PSALM 107:13–14

The highest condition of the human will is when, not seeing God and not seeming to grasp Him at all, it still holds Him fast. Let us then arise in God-born strength every time we feel the darkness closing, or become aware that it has closed around us, and say, "I am of the light and not of the darkness."

Troubled soul, you are not bound to feel, but you are bound to arise. God loves you whether you feel it or not. Try not to feel good when you are not good, but cry to Him who is good. He changes not because you change. No, He has a special tenderness of love toward you because you are in the dark and have no light. His heart is glad when you arise and say, "I will go to my Father" because He sees you through all the gloom through which you cannot see Him. Will to do His will. Say to Him, "My God, I am very dull, low, and discouraged, but you are wise, tender, and strong, and you are my God. I am your child. Forsake me not." Then wait in quietness and faith until light shines into your darkness. Heed not your feelings; heed only your faith.

Reflection

What is the relationship between your feelings and your faith? Why is it important to affirm who God is even when you don't feel His presence—or feel much of anything?

When in Need, Cry Out to God

"Have mercy on me, O LORD, for I am in trouble; my eye wastes away with grief, yes, my soul and my body!"

PSALM 31:9

As God lives by His own will, and we live in Him, so has He given us the power to will in ourselves. How much better would we fare if, finding we have little inclination to seek the source of life, we would still will ourselves upward toward God. How things would improve if we would but call on Him who can fill the emptiest heart, rouse the deadest conscience, quicken the dullest feeling, and strengthen the weakest will!

If ever the time should come, as perhaps it must come to each of us, when all consciousness of well-being will vanish, when the earth will be but a sterile promontory and the heavens a dull congregation of vapors, when God Himself will be but a name and Jesus an old story, even then we can cry out, "My God, My God, why have You forsaken Me?" (Matt. 27:46). And we can, approaching Him with trusting hearts and minds, take up Christ's last words and say, "Father, into Your hands I commit My spirit" (Luke 23:46).

Reflection

When you feel spiritually empty, what do you tend to do? How do you respond to God during such times?

Giving Back to God

"Father, 'into Your hands I commit My spirit.'"

LUKE 23:46

Every highest human act is just a giving back to God of that which He first gave us. "You, God, have given me; here again is your gift." Every act of worship is a holding up to God of what God has made us. "Here, Lord, look what I have; feel with me in what you have made me, in this your own bounty, my being. I am your child."

The last act of our Lord, in commending His spirit at the close of His life, was only a summing up of what He had been doing all His life. He had been offering the sacrifice of Himself all the years, and in thus sacrificing He had lived the divine life. Every morning when He went out before it was day, every evening when He lingered on the shadowed mountain after His friends were gone, He was offering Himself to His Father in the communion of loving words, high thoughts, speechless feelings. In between, He turned to do the same thing in deed, namely, in loving word, in helping thought, in healing action toward His fellows because the way to worship God while the daylight lasts is to work; the service of God, the only "divine service," is the helping of our fellows.

I don't seek to point out this commending of our spirits to the Father as a duty: that will turn the highest privilege we possess into a burden grievous to be borne. But I want to show that it is the simplest, most blessed thing in the human world.

Reflection

What is involved in offering ourselves to God, and how will this affect our willingness to serve other people in His name? Do you agree that every "highest human act" is to give back to God what He first gave us? Why or why not?

Pride: Satan's Weapon

"Pride goes before destruction, and a haughty spirit before a fall."
PROVERBS 16:18

No man alive is beyond the danger of imagining himself exceptional and better than others. If those who think well of themselves were right in so doing, truly the world were ill worth God's making! The silly soul becomes so full of his tempter, and of himself, that he loses interest in all else, cares for nobody but self, and prizes nothing but regard from others.

For the person with rampant pride, God is nowhere, pushed aside and out of the way. And the fellow man becomes like a buzzing fly—else no more to be regarded than a speck of dust neither upon his person nor his garment. This terrible disintegration of life rises out of the most wonderful, mysterious, beautiful, and profound relation in humanity. Its roots go down in the very depths of God; out of its foliage creeps the old serpent and the worm that never dies!

Reflection

Ponder areas of your life in which pride seeks to surface. Do you permit pride to take root in your life or renounce it through the power of God?

Come to God as You Are

"If you then, being evil, know how to give good gifts to your children, how much more will your heavenly Father give the Holy Spirit to those who ask Him!"

LUKE 11:13

Think, brothers and sisters, we walk in the air of an eternal Fatherhood. Every uplifting of the heart is a looking up to the Father. Graciousness and truth are around, above, and beneath us, yes, in us. When we are least worthy, then, most tempted, hardest, unkindest, let us yet commend our spirits into His hands.

How the earthly father would love a child who would creep into his room with a troubled face and sit down at his feet, saying when asked what he wanted, "I feel so naughty, papa, and I want to get good." Would he say to his child, "How dare you! Go away, and be good, and then come to me"? Will we dare to think God would send us away if we came thus? Would He not be pleased that we came, even if we were as angry as Jonah? Would we not let all the tenderness of our nature flow forth on such a child? And will we dare to think that if we, being evil, know how to give good gifts to our children, God will not give us His Spirit when we come to ask Him? Will not some heavenly dew descend cool on the hot anger? Some genial raindrop descend on the dry selfishness? Some glance of sunlight on the cloudy hopelessness? Bread, at least, will be given, and not a stone; water, at least, will be sure, and not vinegar mingled with gall.

Reflection

The next time you are having a difficult day and not responding well to life's challenges, pause to spend a few moments with God. Confess your weaknesses and ask Him to strengthen you and give you joy.

Empowered to Love

"You shall love your neighbor as yourself."
MATTHEW 22:39

The original Scripture here quoted by our Lord is found in the words of God to Moses: "You shall love your neighbor as yourself: I am the LORD" (Lev. 19:18). Our Lord never thought it necessary to be original when He could cite Scriptures that served His purpose.

"Who is my neighbor?" said the lawyer (Luke 10:29). And the Lord taught him that everyone to whom he could be, or for whom he could do, anything was his neighbor. Therefore, each member of the race, as he comes within the touch of one tentacle of our nature, is our neighbor.

The man who will love his neighbor can do so by no mere exercise of the will. The man fulfilled of God, and filled with the Spirit, is empowered to love his fellow man as himself. In God alone can man meet man with undiluted charity and loving-kindness. Our own will and best intentions are insufficient. But when the mind of Christ becomes our mind, when the heart of God becomes our heart, then and then alone can we fulfill the commandment to love our neighbor as ourselves.

Reflection

Do you believe that a person who does not know God can love his neighbor as himself? Why or why not? Which of your "neighbors" might God want you to love in a special way this week?

Questions about Conflict

—◦◦◦—

"The fruit of righteousness is sown in peace by those who make peace."
JAMES 3:18

We must each ask ourselves this question: "Is my neighbor indeed my enemy, or am I my neighbor's enemy, and therefore perceive him to be mine?" Awful thought! "Or, if he is my enemy, am not I his? Am I not refusing to acknowledge the child of the kingdom within his bosom, thus killing the child of the kingdom within my own?"

Let us each claim for ourselves no more indulgence than we give him. Such honesty will end in severity at home and clemency abroad. We are accountable for the ill in ourselves and have to kill it—and for the good in our neighbor, and have to cherish it. He only, in the name and power of God, can kill the bad in himself; we can cherish the good in him by being good to it across all the evil fog that comes between our love and his good. Nor ought we to forget that this fog is often the result of misapprehension and mistake, giving rise to all kinds of indignations, resentments, and regrets.

Scarcely anything about us is just as it seems, but at the core there is truth enough to dispel all falsehood and reveal life as unspeakably divine.

Reflection

Why is it important for each of us to review our attitudes and actions when evaluating difficult relationships with other people? Which key points did the author want to make through this reading?

The Power of Obedient Love

*"May the Lord make you increase and
abound in love to one another and to all."*

1 THESSALONIANS 3:12

M an is a whole. As soon as he unites himself by obedient action, the truth in him makes itself known to him, shining from the new whole. When a man's will once begins to aspire, it will soon find that action must precede feeling in order for him to know the foundation of feeling.

With those who recognize no authority as the ground of tentative action, a doubt, a suspicion of truth, ought to be ground enough for putting it to the test. The whole system of divine education regarding the relationship between man and man has for its end that a man should love his neighbor as himself. It is not a lesson he can learn by itself or a duty the obligation of which can be shown by argument, any more than the difference between right and wrong can be defined in other terms than their own.

The human race generally has gotten as far as recognizing right and wrong; therefore, most men are born capable of making the distinction. The race has not yet lived long enough for its latest offspring to be born with the perception of the truth of loving the neighbor. It is to be seen by the present individual only after a long reception of and submission to the education of life. And once seen, it is believed.

Reflection

Why do we need to love others out of obedience to God rather than waiting until we feel like loving them? What's the relationship between truth and taking action based on the truth?

Earthly and Heavenly Bodies

"For as in Adam all die, even so in Christ all shall be made alive."
1 CORINTHIANS 15:22

This body of ours is the means of revelation to us, the camera in which God's eternal shows are set forth. By the body we come into contact with nature, with our fellow men, with all their revelations of God to us. Through the body we receive all the lessons of passion, suffering, love, beauty, and science. Through the body we are trained outward from ourselves and driven inward into our deepest selves to find God.

We cannot yet have learned all we are meant to learn through the body. How much of the teaching even of this world can the most diligent and most favored man have exhausted before he is called to leave it! Is all that remains to be lost?

We need not only a body to convey revelation to us, but a body to reveal us to others. The thoughts, feelings, and imaginations that arise in us must have their garments of revelation whereby the unseen world within us will be manifested to our brothers and sisters around us; otherwise each is left in human loneliness. Now, if this be one of the uses my body served on earth, the new body must be the same body, glorified as we are glorified, with all that was distinctive of each from his fellows more visible than ever before. The accidental, nonessential, unrevealing, and incomplete will have vanished. That which made the body what it was in the eyes of those who loved us will be tenfold there. Will not this be the resurrection of the body? Of the same body though not of the same dead matter? Every eye will see the beloved. Every heart will cry, "My own again— more mine because it's more himself than ever I beheld him!"

Reflection

What do you think heaven will be like? Why is it important for each of us to keep in mind our future in heaven? How might thinking about heaven influence how we live on earth?

Delight in Doing the Father's Will

"I do not seek My own will but the will of the Father who sent Me."

JOHN 5:30

The joy of the Lord's life, that which made it life to Him, was the Father. Of Him Jesus was always thinking, to Him Jesus was always turning. I suppose most men have some thought of pleasure, satisfaction, or strength to which they turn when action pauses, life becomes still for a moment, and the wheel sleeps on its own swiftness. Jesus needed no pause of action, no rush of renewed consciousness to send Him home; His thought was ever and always His Father. His life was hid in God.

Jesus didn't enter the world for Himself—to establish His own power over the doings, His own influence over men's hearts. He came that they might know the Father who was His joy, His life. The sons of men were His Father's children like Himself. That the Father should have them all in His bosom was the one thought of Jesus' heart; that should be His doing for His Father, cost Him what it might! Jesus came to do His Father's will. Jesus was not interested in Himself, but in His Father and His Father's children. He was there to let men see the goodness of the Father in whom He gloried. For that He entered the weary dream of the world.

Reflection

What does this reading reveal to you about Jesus and His commitment to pursue His Father's will? What is the will of God for *you*? How deeply do you desire that other people will know the Father?

Walking God's Narrow Path

*"Narrow is the gate and difficult is the way which
leads to life, and there are few who find it."*

MATTHEW 7:14

M any are content with themselves because they side with
those whose ways they do not endeavor to follow. Such
are most who call themselves Christians. If men admired themselves only for what they did, their conceit would be greatly
moderated.

Reflection

Think about your thoughts and actions. Are you fully committed to obeying God as revealed in His Word? Why is easy to
"coast," to not be fully committed to walking in the ways of
God?

Live by Faith

"The just shall live by his faith."

HABAKKUK 2:4

Fools must experience a thing themselves before they will believe it. And then, remaining fools, they wonder why their children will not heed their testimony. Faith is the only charm by which the experience of one becomes a vantage ground for the start of another.

One of the hardest demands on the obedience of faith is *to do nothing*. It is often so much easier to do foolishly.

Reflection

Which aspects of faith are the hardest for you? Why?

The Source of Jesus' Goodness

"Now behold, one came and said to Him, 'Good Teacher, what good thing shall I do that I may have eternal life?' So He said to him, 'Why do you call Me good? No one is good but One, that is, God.'"

MATTHEW 19:16–17

The Lord's greatness consisted in His Father being greater than He: The one who calls into being is greater than the one who is called. The Father was always the Father, the Son always the Son. Yet the Son is not of Himself, but by the Father; He does not live by His own power, like the Father. If there were no Father, there would be no Son. All that is the Lord's is the Father's, and all that is the Father's He has given to the Son. The Lord's goodness is of the Father's goodness; because the Father is good, the Son is good. When the word "good" enters the ears of the Son, His heart lifts it at once to His Father, the Father of all.

Jesus' words contain no denial of goodness in Himself. In His grand self-regard, He was not the original of His goodness, nor did He care for His own goodness except to be good. But for His Father's goodness, He would spend life, suffering, labor, and death to make that known! The Father's other children must learn to give Him his due and love Him as did the primal Son! The Father was all in all to the Son, and the Son no more thought of His own goodness than an honest man thinks of his honesty. When the good man sees goodness, he thinks of his own evil. Jesus had no evil to think of, but neither does He think of His goodness; He delights in His Father's.

Reflection

What insights did you gain from this reading concerning God the Father and God the Son? How can the goodness in your life better reflect God's goodness?

A Question of Eternal Life

"What shall I do that I may inherit eternal life?"

MARK 10:17

It is unnecessary to inquire precisely what the youth meant by "eternal life." Whatever shape the thing took to him, it represented something he needed and didn't have—something that, it was clear to him, could be gained only by some path of good. But he thought to gain that thing by *doing*, when the very thing desired was *being*. He would have that as a possession that must possess him.

The Lord cared neither for isolated truth nor for orphaned deed. It was truth in the inward parts, it was the good heart, the motivation of good deeds that He cherished. It was the live, active, knowing, breathing good He came to further. He didn't care for any speculation in morals or religion. It was good men He cared about, not notions of good things or even good actions, except as the outcome of life. Could Jesus by one word have set to rest all the questionings of philosophy as to the supreme good and the absolute truth, I venture to say that word He would not have spoken. But He would die to make men good and true. His whole heart would respond to the cry of the sad publican or despairing Pharisee, "How am I to be good?"

Reflection

Why did He care about a person's heart, not isolated truths and actions? In the Christian life, what is the relationship between *doing* and *being*?

Motivation for Loving the Unlovable

"Love your enemies, do good to those who hate you."
LUKE 6:27

W hy should we love our enemies? The deepest reason for this we cannot put in words because it lies in the absolute reality of their being, where our enemies are of one nature with us, even of the divine nature. The very words *humane* and *humanity* denote some shadow of that loving-kindness that, when perfected after the divine fashion, will include even our enemies.

But how can we love a man or a woman who is cruel and unjust to us? Who is mean, unlovely, carping, uncertain, self-righteous, self-seeking, and self-admiring? These things cannot be loved. The best man hates them most; the worst man cannot love them. But are these the man? Does a woman bear that form in virtue of these? Lies there not within the man and woman a divine element of brotherhood, of sister-hood, a something lovely and lovable—slowly fading, it may be, dying away under the fierce heat of vile passions or the yet more fearful cold of sepulchral selfishness—but there?

Shall we leave our brother to his desolate fate? Shall we not rather say, "With my love at least will you be surrounded, for you lack your own lovingness to enfold you. Love will come as near you as it may, and when your love comes forth to meet mine, we will be one in the indwelling God"? Begin to love him now, and help him into the loveliness that is his.

Reflection

Why is it important to love those who are unlovable—including enemies? How can we learn to recognize the divine spark in such people?

The Detriments of Distrust

*"The LORD is my rock and my fortress and my deliverer;
the God of my strength, in whom I will trust."*

2 SAMUEL 22:2–3

Distrust is atheism and the barrier to all growth. Lord, we don't understand you because we do not trust your Father to be wholehearted toward us. While we who are evil would die to give our children bread to eat, we are not certain the only completely loving Father will care for our every need!

Surely, we let many a whisper of the watching Spirit slip through by brooding over a need that hasn't yet come to us. Tomorrow makes today's whole head sick, its whole heart faint. When we should be still, we fret instead about tomorrow.

Not so do you, Lord! You do the work of your Father. Were you to be like us, we would have good cause to be troubled. But you know it is difficult, things pressing upon every sense, to believe that the informing power of them is in the unseen; that out of it they come; that, where we can discern no hand directing, a will, nearer than any hand, is moving them from within, causing them to fulfill His Word! Help us to obey ... to trust.

Reflection

Do you agree that "distrust is atheism"? Why or why not? Why is distrust in God a barrier to all spiritual growth?

Reflections on Heaven

"The LORD is in His holy temple, the LORD's throne is in heaven;
His eyes behold, His eyelids test the sons of men."

PSALM 11:4

If God has a way, then that is the only way. Every little thing in which you would have your own way has a mission for your redemption, and He will treat you as a disobedient child until you take your Father's way for yours.

There will be this difference, however, between the rich man who loves his riches and the poor man who hates his poverty. When they die, the heart of the one will be still crowded with things and their pleasures, while the heart of the other will be relieved of their lack. The one has had his good things, the other his evil things. But the rich man who held his things lightly nor let them nestle in his heart, who was a channel and no cistern, who was ever and always forsaking his money—starts, in the new world, side by side with the man who accepted, not hated, his poverty. Each will say, "I am free!"

The only air of the soul, in which it can breathe and live, is the present God and the spirits of the just—that is our heaven, our home. Cleansed of greed, jealousy, vanity, pride, possession, and all the thousand forms of evil self, we will be God's children on the hills and in the fields of that heaven, no one desiring to be better than another.

Reflection

Is there any area in which you are not pursuing God's way for your life? What kind of lessons has He been teaching you about becoming more like Jesus and anticipating an eternity in heaven?

When We Reach the End of Ourselves

———◦◦◦———

"O wretched man that I am! Who will deliver me from this body of death? I thank God—through Jesus Christ our Lord!"

ROMANS 7:24–25

He who is made in the image of God must know Him or be desolate. The child must have the Father! Witness the dissatisfaction, indeed desolation, of my wretched soul, alone, unfinished, without Him. It cannot act from itself, except in God. Acting from what seems itself without God is no action at all; it is a mere yielding to impulse. All within is disorder and spasm. There is a cry behind me and a voice before; instincts of betterment tell me I must rise above my present self—perhaps even above all my possible self.

Shall I not tell God my troubles—how He, even He, has troubled me by making me? How unfit I am to be that which I am? That my being is not to me a good thing yet? That I need a law that will reveal to me how I am to make it a good, how I am to be a good and not an evil? Shall I not tell him that I need Him to comfort me, His breath to move on the face of the waters of the chaos He has made? Shall I not cry to Him to be in me rest and strength? To deliver me from my sins and make me clean and glad? Such a cry is of the child to the Father. Every need of God, lifting up the heart, is a seeking of God, is a begging for himself, is profoundest prayer and the root and inspirer of all other prayer.

Reflection

How hungry are you to know God and receive His help? How can you lean more on God's power and strength—and less on your own?

Where Prayers Rest

"Now when He had taken the scroll, the four living creatures and the twenty-four elders fell down before the Lamb, each having a harp, and golden bowls full of incense, which are the prayers of the saints."

REVELATION 5:8

Sad-hearted, be at peace: the snowdrop lies
    Buried in sepulchre of ghastly snow;
But spring is floating up the southern skies,
    And darkling the pale snowdrop waits below.

Let me persuade: in dull December's day
    We scarce believe there is a month of June;
But up the stairs of April and of May
    The hot sun climbeth to the summer's noon.

Yet hear me: I love God, and half I rest.
    O better! God loves thee, so all rest thou.
He is our summer, our dim-visioned Best—
    And in his heart thy prayer is resting now.

Reflection

Why can we be sure that God loves each of us dearly and treasures our prayers? Thank God today that he receives your prayers with utmost care and concern.

One Lovely Morning

"We love Him because He first loved us."
1 John 4:19

One lovely morning, when the green corn lay soaking in the yellow sunlight, and the sky rose above the earth deep and pure and tender like the thought of God about it, Alec became suddenly aware that life was good and the world beautiful. The tide flowed into his chamber like Pactolus, all golden with sunbeams. So easily can God make a man happy! The past had dropped from him like a wild but weary and sordid dream. He was reborn, a new child, in a new bright world, with a glowing summer to revel in.

One of God's lyric prophets, the lark, was within earshot, pouring down a vocal summer of jubilant melody. The lark thought nobody was listening but his wife, but God heard in heaven and the young prodigal heard on earth. He would be a good child henceforth, for one bunch of sunrays was enough to be happy upon.

His mother entered. She saw the beauty upon her boy's worn countenance; she saw the noble watching love on that of his friend; her own filled with light, and she stood transfixed and silent. Annie entered, gazed for a moment, fled to her own room, and burst into adoring tears. For she had seen the face of God, and that face was Love—love like the human, only deeper, deeper—tenderer, lovelier, stronger.

Reflection

What are some of the ways in which God reveals His love to you? What ordinary, daily scenes or events assure you of His love?

Seasons of Change

*"Unless you ... become as little children,
you will by no means enter the kingdom of heaven."*

MATTHEW 18:3

It is not the high summer alone that is God's. All man's winters are His—the winter of our sorrow, the winter of our unhappiness, even "the winter of our discontent." Winter does not belong to death, although the outside of it looks like death. Beneath the snow, the grass is growing. Below the frost, the roots are warm and alive. Winter is only a spring too weak and feeble for us to see that it is living. The cold does for all things what the gardener has sometimes to do for valuable trees: he must half kill them before they will bear any fruit. Winter is in truth the small beginnings of the spring.

Winter is the childhood of the year. Into this childhood of the year came the child Jesus; and into this childhood of the year must we all descend. It is as if God spoke to each of us according to our need: "My son, my daughter, you are growing old and cunning; you must be as a child again. You are growing old and selfish; you must become a child. You are growing old and careful; you must become a child. You are becoming old and distrustful; you must become a child. You are growing old and petty, and weak and foolish; you must become a child—My child, like the baby there, that strong sunrise of faith and hope and love, lying in His mother's arms in the stable."

Reflection

What, specifically, does it mean to have "faith like a child"? In what ways might you need to become like a child?

Nature Reveals the God of the Bible

*"Whatever the Lord pleases He does, in heaven and in earth,
in the seas and in all deep places. He causes the vapors to
ascend from the ends of the earth; He makes lightning for the rain;
He brings the wind out of His treasuries."*

PSALM 135:6–7

What has nature in common with the Bible and its meta-physics? She has a thousand things. The very wind on my face seems to rouse me to fresh effort toward a pure, healthy life. Then there is the sunrise! There is the snowdrop in the snow! There is the butterfly! There is the rain in summer and the clearing of the sky after a storm! There is the hen gathering her chickens under her wing! I begin to doubt whether the commonplace exists anywhere, except in our own mistrusting nature, that will cast no care upon the Unseen.

Reflection

In what ways do the things of nature link with the Bible and its revelation of the Creator? For which things in nature are you especially thankful?

Working with God

*"He who has begun a good work in you will
complete it until the day of Jesus Christ."*

PHILIPPIANS 1:6

If I can put one touch of a rosy sunset into the life of any man or woman under my care, I will feel that I have worked with God. He is in no hurry. If I do what I may in earnest, I need not mourn if I accomplish no great work on the earth. Let God make His sunsets; I will mottle my little fading cloud. To help the growth of a thought that struggles toward the light; to brush with gentle hand the earth-stain from the white of one snowdrop—such be my ambition! So will I scale the rocks in front, not leave my name carved on those behind me.

Reflection

How is this type of thinking different from the views of many people today? What did the author mean when he mentioned scaling the rocks in front, not leaving his name on rocks behind?

Life Awakens Life

"Blessed are those who hear the word of God and keep it!"
LUKE 11:28

The stimulation of imitation is not the life of the Spirit; the use of form where love is not is killing. And if anyone is desirous of spreading the truth, let him apply himself to doing it. Not obeying the truth, he is doubly a liar pretending to teach it. If he obeys it already, let him obey it more.

It is life that awakens life. All form of persuasion is empty except in vital association with reigning obedience. Talking and not doing is dry rot.

Reflection

What is meant by the phrase, "It is life that awakens life"? Why is obedience so important in the spreading of truth?

The Other Side of Sorrow

*"Our light affliction, which is but for a moment, is working
for us a far more exceeding and eternal weight of glory,
while we do not look at the things which are seen, but at the
things which are not seen. For the things which are seen are
temporary, but the things which are not seen are eternal."*

2 CORINTHIANS 4:17–18

In thinking about the miseries and wretchedness in the world,
we too seldom think about the other side. We hear of an
event in association with some certain individual, and we say,
"How dreadful! How miserable!" And perhaps we say, "Is
there, can there be, a God when such a thing takes place?"

But we do not go into the region of actual suffering or conflict. We do not see the heart where the shock falls. We neither
see the proud bracing of energies to meet the rain that threat-
ens, nor the gracious faint in the weak escape from writhing.
We do not see the abatement of pain that is paradise to the tortured. We do not see the gentle upholding in sorrow that comes
even from the ministrations of nature—not to speak of human
nature—to delicate souls.

In a word, we do not see, and the sufferer himself does not
understand, how God is present every moment, comforting,
upholding, heeding that the pain will not be more than can be
borne, making the thing possible and not hideous.

Reflection

What perspective does this reading provide on human suffering? How can we know God is with us, even though we don't see His hand or feel His presence?

Live a Life of Love

"Love one another; as I have loved you, that you
also love one another. By this all will know that you are
My disciples, if you have love for one another."

JOHN 13:34–35

Love is the first comforter, and where love and truth speak, the love will be felt where the truth is never perceived. Love indeed is the highest in all truth; and the pressure of a hand, a kiss, the caress of a child, will often do more to persuade than the wisest argument, even rightly understood. Love alone is wisdom, love alone is power. Where love seems to fail, it is where self has stepped between and dulled the potency of its rays.

Reflection

Why is godly love so powerful? Why do people who aren't Christians respond to love yet will not respond as openly to biblical truth? In what ways might you demonstrate love to someone today?

The Sleeping Tyrant Within

"I know that in me (that is, in my flesh) nothing good dwells."

ROMANS 7:18

What we call degeneracy is often but the unveiling of what was there all the time, and the evil we could become, we are. If I have in me the tyrant or the miser, there he is, and such am I—as surely as if the tyrant or the miser were even now visible to the wondering dislike of my neighbors. I do not say the characteristic is so strong or would be so hard to change us by the revealing development it must become; but it is there, latent but alive, sleeping but ready to awaken.

Only by the power of God, working in heart and mind, can we subdue the slumbering tyrant within. Only by the Holy Spirit's prevailing strength can we restrain the evil desires seeking to spring forth. Within each person, a battle rages; only through God is victory secured.

Reflection

Why must you, in the power of God, face and overcome the evil desires within you? What are the consequences if we ignore the evil inside us?

Serve Others, Not Self

"Know this, that in the last days perilous times will come: For men will be lovers of themselves."

2 TIMOTHY 3:1–2

To try to make other people comfortable is the only way to get comfortable ourselves, and that comes partly by not being able to think so much about ourselves when we are helping other people. Our selves will always do pretty well if we don't pay them too much attention. They are like some little children who will be happy enough as long as they are left to their own games. But when we begin to interfere with them and indulge them extravagant playthings or too many sweets, they begin at once to act haughty and spoiled.

Reflection

Do you find it easy or hard to help other people? How much time and energy do you put into others—and how much into yourself?

Keep Reaching Forward

"We desire that each one of you show the same diligence to the full assurance of hope until the end, that you do not become sluggish, but imitate those who through faith and patience inherit the promises."

HEBREWS 6:11–12

They belong to the common class of mortals who, although they are weaving a history, are not aware of it, and in whom the process goes on so slowly that the eye of the artist can find in them no substance sufficient to be woven into a human creation in tale or poem. How dull that life looks to him, with its ambitions, its tasks, its chores, its dinners, its sermons, its tailor's bills, its weariness over all—without end or goal save that toward which it is driven purposeless!

Not until a hope is born such that its fulfillment depends on the will of him who cherishes it, does a man begin to develop the stuff out of which a tale can be wrought. For then he begins to have a story of his own—it may be for good, it may be for evil—but a story nonetheless.

Reflection

Why do so many people travel through life with little enthusiasm or excitement? What keeps you looking ahead and moving forward?

The Consequences of Unforgiveness

―◦◦◦◦―

"Whenever you stand praying, if you have anything against anyone, forgive him, that your Father in heaven may also forgive you your trespasses. But if you do not forgive, neither will your Father in heaven forgive your trespasses."

MARK 11:25–26

It may be an infinitely less evil to murder a man than to refuse to forgive him. The former may be the act of a moment of passion; the latter is the heart's choice. It is spiritual murder, the worst, to hold on to hate, nurse grudges, and brood over wrongs committed. We listen to the voice of our own hurt pride or hurt affection (only the latter without the suggestion of the former thinks no evil) to the injury of the evildoer. In as far as we can, we quench the relations of life between us; we close up the passages of possible return. This shuts out God, our life-giver and life-sustainer. For how are we to receive the forgiving presence while we shut out our brother from our portion of the universal forgiveness, the final restoration, thus refusing to let God be all in all?

If God appeared to us, how could He say, "I forgive you," while we remained unforgiving to our neighbor? Suppose it possible that He should say so. His forgiveness would be no good to us while we were uncured of our unforgiveness. It would not touch us. It would not come near us. No, it would hurt us, for we would think ourselves safe and well while the horror of disease was eating the heart out of us.

Reflection

Why do you think God takes unforgiveness so seriously? Does anyone come to mind whom you need to forgive?

Wait with Expectation

*"Let patience have its perfect work, that you may
be perfect and complete, lacking nothing."*

JAMES 1:4

As long as I can remember, my heart was given to expectation, was tuned to long waiting. Would they not tell me that such expectation was but the shadow of the cloud of love, hanging no bigger than a man's hand on the far horizon, but fraught with storm for mind and soul, which, when it withdrew, would carry with it the glow and the glory and the hope of life; bring at best but the mirage of an unattainable paradise, therefore direst of deceptions! Little do such people suspect that their own behavior has withered their faith and that their unbelief has dried up their life. They can now no more believe in what they once felt than a cloud can believe in the rainbow it once bore on its bosom.

Reflection

What role does patient waiting have in the development and nurture of spiritual faith? In what ways has unbelief and wrong behavior dried up your life and withered your faith?

God's Ongoing Revelation

"[In Christ] are hidden all the treasures of wisdom and knowledge."
COLOSSIANS 2:3

The Bible leads us to Jesus—the inexhaustible, ever-unfolding revelation of God. It is Christ "in whom are hidden all the treasures of wisdom and knowledge," not the Bible, save as leading to Him. And why are we told that these treasures are hidden in Him who is the revelation of God? Is it that we should despair of finding them and cease to seek them? Are they not hidden in Him so that they may be revealed to us in due time—that is, when we need them? Is He not the Truth—the Truth to men? Is he not the High Priest of His brethren, to answer all the troubled questionings that arise in their dim humanity?

Certainly, there may be things that the mere passing into another stage of existence will illuminate, but the questions that come here must be inquired into here, and if not answered here, then there too until they be answered. There is more hidden in Christ than we will ever learn, here or there either, but those who begin first to inquire will soonest be gladdened with revelation; and with them He will be best pleased, for the slowness of His disciples troubled him. To say that we must wait for the other world in order to know the mind of Him who came to this world to give Himself to us seems to me the foolishness of a worldly, lazy spirit. The Son

of God is the teacher of men, giving to them of His Spirit—
that Spirit who manifests the deep things of God, being to a
man the mind of Christ.

Reflection

How deeply do you desire to know the deep things of God?
Which questions might you ask God, for which He can reveal
answers through the Holy Spirit, biblical revelation, and other
believers?

Overflowing Love

*"Walk in love, as Christ also has loved us and given Himself for us,
an offering and a sacrifice to God for a sweet-smelling aroma."*

EPHESIANS 5:2

The world little knows what power is given the man who simply and really believes in Him who is the Savior and able to save men from their sins! He may be neither wise nor prudent. He may be narrow and dim-sighted even in the things he loves best; they may promise him much, and yield him but a poor fragment of the joy that might be and ought to be his. He may present them to others clothed in no attractive hues or in any word of power. And yet if he has but that love for his neighbor that is rooted in, and springs from, love for his God, he is always a redeeming, reconciling influence among his fellows.

Reflection

Why is "simple" belief so powerful, despite what some people who elevate the intellect say about this? Why is powerful love for our neighbors rooted in our love for God?

Our Deepest Hopes
Lead Us to God

"I will hope continually, and will praise You yet more and more."

PSALM 71:14

It is this formless idea of something at hand that keeps men and women striving to tear from the bosom of the world the secret of their own hopes. How little they know that what they look for in reality is their God! This is that for which their heart and their flesh cry out.

Lead me on, my hopes. I know that you are true and not vain. Vanish from my eyes day after day, but arise in new forms. I will follow your holy deception—follow until you have brought me to the feet of my Father in heaven, where I will find you all with folded wings spangling the sapphire dusk whereon stands His throne, which is our home.

Reflection

Which hopes are drawing you closer to God? What will be required to take action related to those hopes?

Obey ... and Shine!

"Whoever keeps His word, truly the love of God is perfected in him."

1 JOHN 2:5

There was a secret between them (Andrew and Dawtie)—a secret proclaimed on the housetops, a secret hidden, the most precious of pearls, in their hearts—that the earth is the Lord's and the fullness thereof; that its work is the work of the Lord, whether the sowing of the field, the milking of the cow, the giving to the poor, the spending of wages, the reading of the Bible; that God is all in all, and every throb of gladness His gift; that their life came fresh every moment from His heart; that what was lacking to them would arrive the very moment He had gotten them ready for it. They were God's little ones in God's world.... Among poverty-stricken Christians, consumed with care to keep a hold of the world and save their souls, they were as two children of the house. By living in the presence of the Living One, they had become themselves His presence—dim lanterns through which His light shone steady. Whoever obeys, shines.

Reflection

Do you agree that the Lord's work involves all aspects of daily life? Are you obeying God in *every* area of life so that His light can shine steadily through you?

The Inspiration of Creation

"I will open rivers in desolate heights, and fountains in the midst of the valleys ... that they may see and know, and consider and understand together, that the hand of the LORD has done this, and the Holy One of Israel has created it."

ISAIAH 41:18, 20

Nobody quite knows the beauty of a country, especially of a quiet country, except one who has been born in it, or for whom at least childhood and youth have opened door after door into the hidden phases of its life. There is no square yard on the face of this earth, but someone can in part understand what God meant in making it. The same changeful skies canopy the most picturesque and dullest landscapes; the same winds wake and blow over desert and pasture lands, making the bosoms of young and old swell with the delight of their blowing.

Reflection

Which aspects of nature particularly touch your heart? Set aside some time soon to enjoy the beauty of God's creation and praise Him for the meaning He gives to earthly life.

The Fullness of God's Forgiveness

"Through the LORD's mercies we are not consumed."

LAMENTATIONS 3:22

Many people, weighed down by past sins, cannot comprehend the full power of God's forgiveness to relieve the burdened heart and troubled conscience. They say, "Even God cannot erase the fact of my misdeeds. He cannot undo what I have done." These people care more about their own cursed shame than their Father's blessed love! Such would rather persist in self-condemnation than accept God's purifying mercy.

When a person genuinely confesses, trusting in the power of the Savior's blood, the truth sets him free. He knows that the shackles have been removed and the death sentence lifted. He is convinced that God's forgiveness obliterates sin's ability to condemn and consume.

Reflection

Why is it sometimes difficult to accept God's forgiveness? What does it mean that we are "not consumed" because of God's mercies?

In God's Hands

"The LORD is my strength and song, and He has become my salvation."
PSALM 118:14

Malcolm's spirits kept rising as they bowled along over the bright cold waters. He never felt so capable as when at sea. His energies had been first called out in combat with the elements, and hence he always felt strongest, most at home, and surest of himself on the water. Young as he was, however, such had been his training under Mr. Graham, that a large part of this elevation of spirit was owing to an unreasoned sense of being there more immediately in the hands of God. Later in life, he interpreted the mental condition thus—that of course he was always and in every place equally in God's hands, but that at sea he felt the truth more keenly. Where a man has nothing firm under him, where his life depends on winds invisible and waters unstable, where a single movement may be death, he learns to feel what is at the same time just as true every night he spends asleep in the bed in which generations have slept before him, or any sunny hour he spends walking over ancestral acres.

Reflection

When do you feel the strongest sense of God's presence? When do you feel distant from Him—and how do you respond when that happens?

Do the Right Thing

"Whatever you do, do all to the glory of God."
1 CORINTHIANS 10:31

When you have a thing to do, you will do it in right proportion to your love of right. But do the right thing, and you will love the right thing, for by doing it you will see it in a measure as it is, and no one can see the truth as it is without loving it. The more you *talk* about what is right, or even about the doing of it, the more you are in danger of exemplifying how loosely theory may be allied to practice. Talk without action saps the very will. Something you have to do is waiting undone. The only refuge is to *do*.

Reflection

In which areas of your life might God want you to "do the right thing"? What is your guideline for doing what is right?

Do Not Serve Riches

"He who trusts in his riches will fall."
PROVERBS 11:28

What does it mean for a person to "serve" riches? When he feels he cannot be happy without them. When he puts forth the energies of his nature to get them. When he schemes and dreams and lies awake thinking about them. When he will not give to his neighbor for fear of becoming poor himself. When he wants to have more, and to know he has more, than he can possibly need.

Still more is he mammon's slave when his devotion to his god makes him oppressive to those over whom his wealth gives him power, or when he becomes unjust in order to add to his stores. How will it be with such a man when suddenly he finds that the world has vanished, and he is alone with God? There lies the body in which he used to live, whose poor necessities first made money of value to him, but with which itself and its fictitious value are both left behind. He cannot even now try to bribe God with a check. The angels will not bow down to him because his property, as set forth in his will, takes five or six figures to express its amount. It makes no difference to them that he has lost it, though, because they never respected him. And the poor souls of Hades, who envied him the wealth they had lost before, rise up as one man to welcome him, not for love of him—no worshipper of Mammon loves another—but rejoicing in the mischief that has befallen him.

Reflection

Contrast the thoughts presented here with the prevailing thoughts of our culture. Why does money so easily become the master?

104

Simple Contentment

"Godliness with contentment is great gain."
1 TIMOTHY 6:6

It is a great thing to have the greetings of the universe presented in fire and food. Let me, if I may, be ever welcomed to my room in winter by a glowing hearth and in summer by a vase of flowers. If I may not, let me then think how nice they would be and bury myself in my work.

I do not think that the road to contentment lies in despising what we have not got. Let us acknowledge all good, all delight that the world holds, and be content without it.

Reflection

How content are you? When have you been most content? Think about that time and compare it to your life today.

On the Potter's Wheel

---

*"The vessel that he made of clay was marred in the hand of the potter;
so he made it again into another vessel, as it seemed good to the
potter to make. Then the word of the LORD came to me, saying:
'O house of Israel, can I not do with you as this potter?'"*

JEREMIAH 18:4–6

No man can order his life, because it comes flowing over
him from behind. But if it lay before us, and we could
watch its current approaching from a long distance, what could
we do with it before it had reached the now?

The one secret of life and development is not to devise and
plan, but to fall in with the forces at work. To do every
moment's duty aright, to jump in and swim along with a strong
current—this will move us forward swiftly. If men would but
believe that they are in the process of creation and consent to
participate—let the Maker handle them as the potter his clay,
yielding themselves in respondent motion and submissive
hopeful action with the turning of his wheel—they would
before long find themselves shaped in the useful form of He
who made them. They would welcome every pressure of that
molding hand upon them, even when it was felt in pain, and
sometimes not only to believe but to recognize the divine end
in view, the bringing of a son into glory. Whereas, behaving like
children who struggle and scream while their mother washes
and dresses them, they find they have to be washed and dressed
notwithstanding, and with the more discomfort. They may even

have to find themselves set half naked and but half dried in a corner to come to their right minds, and ask to be finished.

Reflection

Are you trusting the Potter to form you, or are you trying to rebel against the shaping He is doing in your life? In what ways do you find it difficult to be shaped by the Creator?

Worthy Spiritual Battles

"The Spirit of the Lord is upon Me, because He has anointed Me to preach the gospel to the poor; He has sent Me to heal the brokenhearted, to proclaim liberty to the captives and recovery of sight to the blind, to set at liberty those who are oppressed."

LUKE 4:18

The battle of the warrior is with confused noise and garments rolled in blood, but how much harder and worthier battles are fought, not in shining armor, but amid filth and squalor, physical as well as moral, on a field of wretched and wearisome commonplace?

Reflection

In which commonplace "battles" might God want you to become involved? How are you responding to the physical and spiritual needs of people in your community?

God Waits for an Open Door

"Behold, I stand at the door and knock. If anyone hears My voice and opens the door, I will come in to him and dine with him, and he with Me."

REVELATION 3:20

God will not force open any door in order to enter. He may send a tempest about the house; the wind of His admonishment may burst doors and windows, yes, shake the house to its foundations. But even then He will not enter. The door must be opened by the willing hand, before the foot of love will cross the threshold. He watches to see the door moved from within. Every tempest is but an assault in the siege of love. It is love outside the house that seeks to be inside—love that knows the house is no home, only a lonely place, until it enters. Things must be cast out to make room for the new compassion, life-giving resident.

If a man has courage and encounters the army of bats and snakes that infest the place of the Holy, it is but to find that the task too great for him, that the temple of God will not be cleansed by him, that the very dust he raises in sweeping is full of corruptive forces. Let those who would do what they must yet cannot, would be what they must yet cannot, remember with hope and courage that He who knows all about our being once spoke a parable emphasizing that they ought always to pray, and not to faint (Luke 18:1–5).

Reflection

Why won't God enter a person's heart without an invitation? Who do you know whose door God is waiting to enter? How might you encourage this person to open the door?

Glimpses of Heaven

"Rejoice and be exceedingly glad, for great is your reward in heaven."
MATTHEW 5:12

What a wonderful thing waking is. The time of the ghostly moonlight passes by, and the great positive sunlight comes. A man who dreams, and knows that he is dreaming, thinks he knows what waking is, but knows it so little that he mistakes, one after another, many vague and dim changes in his dream for an awakening. When the true waking comes at last, he is filled and overflowed with the power of its reality.

Likewise, one who in the darkness lies waiting for the light about to be struck and is trying to conceive with all the force of his imagination what the light will be like, is yet, when the reality flames up before him, seized as by a new and unexpected thing, different from and beyond all his imagining. He feels as if the darkness were cast to an infinite distance behind him.

So shall it be with us when we wake from this dream of life into the truer life beyond, and find all our present notions of being thrown back as into a dim, vapory region of dreamland.

Reflection

What do you think heaven—"the truer life beyond"—will be like? Why? What hope should the existence of heaven generate in the hearts and minds of believers?

The Soul's Deep Longing

"O God, You are my God; early will I seek
You; my soul thirsts for You."

PSALM 63:1

There is a strange delight in motion. The hope that the end will bring fresh enjoyment has something to do with it, no doubt. The accompaniments of the motion, the change of scene, the mystery that lies beyond the next hill or the next turn in the road, the breath of the summer wind, the scent of the pine trees especially, and of all the earth, the tinkling jangle of the harness as you pass the trees on the roadside, the life of the horses, the glitter and the shadow, the cottages and the roses and the rosy faces, the scent of burning wood or peat from the chimneys—these and a thousand other things combine to make such a journey delightful. But I believe it needs something more than this, something even closer to the human life, to account for the pleasure that motion gives us.

I suspect it is its living symbolism, the hidden relations that it bears to the eternal soul in its aspirations and longings—ever following after, ever attaining, never satisfied.

Reflection

What do you think is the relationship between motion and our deepest soul yearnings? When will our "eternal souls" be satisfied?

Jesus Is the Truth

―――∞∞∞―――

"I am the way, the truth, and the life.
No one comes to the Father except through Me."

JOHN 14:6

Some would willingly believe that life is but a phantasm, if only it might forever afford them a world of pleasant dreams. Yet to him who has once seen even a shadow only of the truth, and even hoping he has seen it when it is present no longer, tries to obey it—to him the real vision, the Truth Himself—will come, and depart no more, but abide with him forever.

Reflection

What is the difference between relative and absolute truth, and why is the issue of spiritual truth especially important today? Why is it vital to remember that Jesus is the truth?

A Deeper Kind of Faith

"Thomas, because you have seen Me, you have believed.
Blessed are those who have not seen and yet have believed."

JOHN 20:29

Do you count it a great faith to believe what God has said? Can you not believe in God Himself? Or do you not find it so hard to believe what He has said that even that is almost more than you can do? If I ask you why, will not the true answer be: "Because we are not quite sure that He did say it"? If you believed in God, you would find it easy to believe the Word. You would not even need to inquire whether He had said it; you would know that He meant it.

Let us dare something. Let us not always be unbelieving children. The Lord, not forbidding those who insist on seeing before they will believe, blesses those who have not seen and yet have believed. He blesses those who believe without the sight of the eyes and without the hearing of the ears. They are blessed to whom a wonder is not a fable, to whom a mystery is not a mockery, to whom a glory is not an unreality.

Reflection

If God were talking to you face-to-face right now, what would He say about the level of your faith in Him? About your knowledge of His attributes? About your willingness to step out in faith?

Reflections on Getting Older

*"The righteous shall flourish like a palm tree, he shall grow like
a cedar in Lebanon. Those who are planted in the house of
the LORD shall flourish in the courts of our God. They shall
still bear fruit in old age; they shall be fresh and flourishing."*

PSALM 92:12–14

Why shouldn't a man be happy when he is growing old,
so long as his faith strengthens the feeble knees that
chiefly suffer in the process of going down the hill? True, the
fever heat is over and the oil burns more slowly in the lamp of
life. But if there is less fervor, there is more pervading
warmth; if less of fire, more of sunshine. There is less smoke
and more light. Truly, youth is good, but old age is better—to
the man who forsakes not his youth when his youth forsakes
him. The sweet visitations of nature do not depend on youth
or romance, but on that quiet spirit whose meekness inherits
the earth.

The smell of that field of beans gives me more delight now
than ever it could have given me when I was a youth. And if I
ask myself why, I find it is simply because I have more faith now
than I had then. The music of the spheres is mine if old age
should make me deaf as the adder. More and more nature
becomes to me one of God's books of poetry—not His grand-
est, that is history—but His loveliest, perhaps.

Reflection

According to this reading, what causes older people to not only enjoy old age but to flourish? How might the truths found here apply to your life right now, or to someone you love?

Let Love Work in You

"You shall love your neighbor as yourself."

MARK 12:31

It is possible to love our neighbor as ourselves. Our Lord never spoke with hyperbole, although that is the supposition on which many people unconsciously interpret His words, in order to persuade themselves that they believe them. We may see that it is possible before we attain to it because our perceptions of truth are always in advance of our condition. A man who knows that he does not yet love his neighbor as himself may believe in such a condition, may even see that there is no other goal of human perfection, nothing else to which the universe is speeding, propelled by the Father's will. Let him labor on and not faint at the thought that God's day is a thousand years. His millennium is likewise one day—yes, this day, because we have Him who is truly love in us, working even now.

Reflection

Which people—at work, in my neighborhood, among my family—might you love in special ways today? What are some practical ways in which you can demonstrate love to them?

Dwell on Uplifting Things

*"Whatever things are lovely, whatever things are
of good report ... meditate on these things."*

PHILIPPIANS 4:8

We are so easily affected by the smallest things that are unpleasant that we ought to train ourselves to dwell only on encouraging, uplifting things. The unpleasant ones are like the thorns, which make themselves felt as we scramble through the thickets of life. Pricked and scratched by the thorns, we grumble and are blind to everything but them.

The flowers, lovely leaves, red berries, clusters of edible nuts, and birds' nests do not force themselves on our attention as the thorns do, and the thorns make us forget to look for them. But a scratch would be forgotten if we but allowed a moment's repose on any of the quiet, unobtrusive beauties that lie around the half-trodden way, offering their gentle healing. How often on our walk through life do we glare at prickly weeds while failing even to glimpse fields of flowers.

Let us cultivate the friendship of comforting, cheering things. Beauty is one of the surest antidotes to vexation. Often when life looked dreary about me, from some real or fancied injustice or indignity, a thought of truth has been flashed into my mind from a flower, a shape of frost, or even a lingering shadow—not to mention such glories as angel-winged clouds, rainbows, stars, and sunrises.

Reflection

Which small and unpleasant things tend to sidetrack you from appreciating life's blessings? How might you choose to respond differently in order to refocus on positive and lovely things?

God Fulfills Our Dreams

"I know the thoughts that I think toward you, says the LORD,
thoughts of peace and not of evil, to give you a future and a hope."

JEREMIAH 29:11

M an dreams and desires; God designs and wills and quickens.

When a man dreams his own dream, he is at the mercy of his dream, for it may or may never come to fruition. When the Lord gives him a dream, however, He provides all the means and resources to fulfill it.

Reflection

Do you really believe that God not only gives you a dream, but will also fulfill it if you walk obediently with Him? Name two or three of your dreams that you believe are God-inspired.

The Source of True Contentment

"Oh, that men would give thanks to the LORD for His goodness, and for His wonderful works to the children of men! For He satisfies the longing soul, and fills the hungry soul with goodness."

Perhaps the greater part of the energy of this world's life goes forth in the endeavor to rid itself of discomfort. Some, to escape it, leave their natural surroundings behind them and with strong and continuous effort keep rising in the social scale, to discover at every new ascent fresh trouble, as they think, awaiting them, whereas in truth they have brought the trouble with them.

Others, making haste to be rich, are slow to find out that the poverty of their souls, none the less that their purses are filling, will yet keep them unhappy. Some court endless change, nor know that on themselves the change must pass that will set them free. Others expand their souls with knowledge, only to find that content will not dwell in the great house they have built.

People can search, scheme, and scurry around in attempt to find contentment. In the end they will, if enlightened by the Holy Spirit, realize that the only true contentment is provided by a close, consistent relationship with God. It is He and He alone who satisfies the soul.

Reflection

Name some of the typical ways people in our society try to find contentment. What are some of the ways *you* have sought contentment? Do you consider yourself to be content right now?

A Prayer for God's Continual Care

"Lo, I am with you always."
MATTHEW 28:20

Thou in my heart hast planted, gardener divine,
  A scion of the tree of life: it grows;
  But not in every wind or weather it blows;
  The leaves fall sometimes from the baby tree,
  And the life-power seems melting into pine;
  Yet still the sap keeps struggling to the shine,
  And the unseen root clings cramplike unto thee.

Do thou, my God, my spirit's weather control;
  And as I do not gloom though the day be done,
  Let me not gloom when earth-born vapors roll
  Across the infinite zenith of my soul.
  Should sudden brain-frost through the heart's summer run,
  Cold, weary, joyless, waste of air and sun,
  Thou art my south, my summer-wind, my all, my one.

Reflection

Do you sense God's continual care, during good times and gloomy times? What phrases from this poem do you find encouraging?

Stay Focused on Jesus

"My God, My God, why have You forsaken Me?"
MATTHEW 27:46

N ow the foreseen horror has come. Our Lord is drinking the dreaded cup, and the Father's will has vanished from His eyes. Were that will visible in His suffering, His will could bow with tearful gladness under the shelter of its grandeur. But now His will is left alone to drink the cup of the Father's will in torture. In the sickness of this agony, the will of Jesus arises perfect at last; feeling abandoned and utterly alone, He will complete the mission for which He was sent to earth. This is the faith of the Son of God. God withdrew, as it were, so that the perfect will of the Son might arise and go forth to find the Father's will.

But wherein or what can this glorious peak of faith have to do with the creatures who call themselves Christians, creeping about in the valleys, hardly knowing that there are mountains above them, except that they take offense at and stumble over pebbles washed across their path by glacier streams? I will tell you: We are and remain creeping, stumbling Christians when we look at ourselves and not at Christ, because we gaze at the marks of our soiled feet and the trail of our defiled garments instead of up at the snows of purity.

Reflection

What is involved in "looking at Christ" rather than our-selves? Consider three new ways in which you can focus more on Christ this coming week.

The Connection between Love and Mourning

"Blessed are the poor in spirit, for theirs is the kingdom of heaven. Blessed are those who mourn, for they shall be comforted."

MATTHEW 5:3–4

The promise to those who mourn is not *the kingdom of heaven*, but that their mourning will end, that they will be comforted. To mourn is not to fight with evil; it is only to miss that which is good. Mourning is a withered blossom on the rose-tree of love. Is there any mourning worthy of the name that has not love for its root? Men mourn because they love. Love is the life out of which are fashioned all the natural feelings, every emotion of man. Love modeled by faith is hope; love shaped by wrong is anger—indeed anger, though pure of sin. Love invaded by loss is grief.

Reflection

How would you explain the relationship between mourning and love? How have you experienced this relationship in your life?

Don't Worry about Tomorrow

"*Do not worry about tomorrow, for tomorrow will worry about its own things. Sufficient for the day is its own trouble.*"

MATTHEW 6:34

Every minute is a tomorrow to the minute that goes before it and is bound to it by the same duty-roots that make every moment one with eternity. But there is no more occasion to bind minute to minute with the twine of anxiety than to ruin both today and the grand future with the cares of a poor imaginary tomorrow.

Today's duty is the only true provision for tomorrow, and those who are careful about the morrow are but the more likely to bring its troubles on them by that neglect of duty that care always occasions. There are those who say that care for the morrow is what distinguishes the man from the beast; certainly it is one of the many things that distinguish the slave of nature from the child of God.

Reflection

In what ways might you live more for today than tomorrow? How will worrying about tomorrow affect what you do today?

Subject Index

―――❦―――

Scripture Index

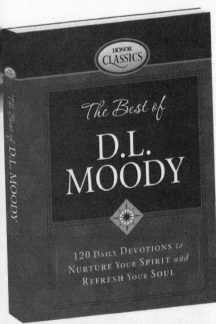

Additional copies of this
and other Honor books are available
wherever good books are sold.

━━━◦◦◦━━━

If you have enjoyed this book, or if it has had an impact on
your life, we would like to hear from you.

Please contact us at:

HONOR BOOKS
Cook Communications Ministries, Dept. 201
4050 Lee Vance View
Colorado Springs, CO 80918

Or visit our Web site: www.cookministries.com

HONOR HB BOOKS
Inspiration and Motivation for the Seasons of Life